BREAK

NEVER BY THE BOOK

KELLY SCHOLS

RENEGADE PRESS

Published by **Renegade Press,** Mount Vernon, WA

ISBN 978-0-578-63384-8

LCCN 2019957174

Printed in the United States of America

Contents

FOREWORD
Kenny Chapman

Have you ever dreamed of being debt free? Have you ever struggled with the challenges of keeping your life on track? Do you want to overcome all odds and finally win in your life? If you can relate to any of these (or similar) questions, then *Never by the Book* is a must-read.

I began my entrepreneurial journey as a struggling drain cleaner with no business being in business. From that life-changing day in 1994, I somehow found myself as a successful entrepreneur who is now the founder and president of The Blue Collar Success Group, a market-leading coaching and training organization focused on home service companies.

Through this work, I met Kelly Schols after one of my keynote presentations in 2012. He bought all of what I was selling and then began implementing with a drive and focus like I'd never seen before. His tenacity was different; his perspective was wise. He had clarity of who he was and why he was here.

What makes this guy so different? I had to know. Our relationship turned from coach-client to friends, then eventually business partners in a few different deals. This eventually led to Kelly joining our Blue Collar Success Group team as a Financial and Accountability Coach.

In this book, Kelly shares his incredible journey. He'll open your eyes. He'll make your eyes water. He'll teach you some things you've heard before and already forgotten. He'll show you that you don't need to do things "by the book" to succeed in life and business.

Kelly guides you through his story and helps you understand how to take what he's lived, learned, and implemented to become financially free and create more options in your life than you could've ever imagined. Do yourself a favor. Make the time to read this book, follow Kelly's lead, and watch your own life improve in any capacity you desire.

Kenny Chapman
Founder and President
The Blue Collar Success Group, Inc.

FOREWORD
Mark Matteson

Kelly and I met because of a kind referral from a colleague. A mutual friend told him, "There's a bestselling author and international speaker right in your backyard you should talk to. He lives right down I-5 in Edmonds!" We had lunch. He heard me speak to my old college. We began a working relationship. I conducted some seminars for his employees. We became friends. Emerson wrote, "If we are related, we shall meet."

When I agreed to read Kelly's book, I thought I knew a great deal about the man. But how well do you really know someone? Yes, he is a successful businessman, a loving father, a widower, an athlete, and a genuinely good guy. Despite his success, I thought him to be humble, authentic, sincere, and affable.

Over coffee in Mt. Vernon, Washington, we talked about what it takes to get a book published and out to the world. I had written five of my own, so I had a few ideas to share. He handed me a manuscript. I promised to read it over the weekend and offer some advice.

I began reading it at 0530 today. I couldn't put it down. His story is riveting. Kelly has been to Hell and back, only to come out with longer legs for bigger strides. If his story doesn't instruct and inspire you, you'd better check your pulse.

Read this book! Give it to your friends and employees. They will thank you. Now I know the man. I have an even deeper and abiding respect for him, in a way I simply did not have before reading his story.

Thank you, Kelly, for baring your soul and telling your extraordinary story of surviving adversity and making a difference in people's lives. We are all better for it.

Mark Matteson
Bestselling author,
Freedom from Fear

INTRODUCTION

I AM NOT SUPPOSED TO BE HERE. After a life-threatening pregnancy, my mother had her tubes tied, a procedure that is a ninety-nine percent effective means of birth control. It's a permanent solution. *But here I am.* I emerged into the world with my umbilical cord wrapped tightly around my neck. *But here I am.* I went on to live a life consumed by alcoholism, bad decisions, self-sabotage, horrible accidents, fistfights, jail cells, heartache, and unimaginable loss. *But here I am.*

On the other hand, my life has also been one of hard work, learning, personal growth, enduring friendships, amazing triumphs, spectacular financial successes, community building, high achievement, boundless love, and giving back more than I've taken. *And here I am.* Not bad for someone who isn't supposed to be here.

How did this happen? If you knew me when I was younger you would never pick me out as someone likely to amount to anything. My classmates didn't name me "Most Likely to Succeed." I didn't go to college. There isn't a person on Earth who thought they'd see my name on a book cover. I didn't do any of the things that successful people do. *I did the opposite.* I partied. I drank. I raised hell. I was the shining example of what not to be when you grow up.

That's what you would have *seen,* but there was more going on under the hood. Regardless of all appearances, I did, in fact, do some of the things that successful people do. I worked like a dog. I took help when it was offered. I changed and adapted when necessary. These were some of the keys that led me to a life that defied the expectations of my peers. Today I am considered to be in the top five percent of the world's most successful people. *Surprise!*

But I am not here just to tell you my story. If that were the case I would tell you to stop reading now! On the contrary, I'm here to help. In many ways, the episodes of my life have been no different than those of millions of other people. And yet things have turned out remarkably well for me. How can you start from wherever you are, even if you're at life's lowest point, and build yourself up to be a person of success and significance, a person who is admired and respected, the kind of person who will make your parents (and your children!) proud? You can do it. I did it. And after a lifetime of dizzying highs and rock-bottom lows I can tell you that I've cracked the code. That's why I'm here; *that's* why I'm telling you my story.

Wherever you are in life, wherever you find yourself, I have some hard-earned wisdom that can take you to the next level. When it comes to teaching, they say that nothing beats experience. I agree, but there are some experiences that you're probably better off not having. No problem; I did it so that you don't have to, and I'm happy to share what I've learned.

I don't do things by the book. I don't follow standard protocol. I've forged my own path. And, with the help of some wonderful people who had faith in me in spite of myself, I've succeeded beyond my wildest dreams.

Before you turn the page, remember that this book only works if you do. It's not enough just to read it. As my story unfolds, you'll see exactly how I turned my life around to become a successful husband, father, and entrepreneur. Be ready to apply the lessons to your own life. Accept the challenge. What worked for me will almost certainly work for you; and while it may not be easy, it will definitely be worth it. Let's get started...

Chapter One

GROWING UP

From day one, my brothers and I were a rowdy bunch.
Being the youngest I always wanted to hang around with
my two older brothers, and there wasn't much that I
wouldn't do if they pushed me. When I was nine months
old Mom found my brothers cooking slugs in the oven.
They said they were feeding them to me for a snack. To
this day I wonder if I ate them. This was the first episode
of many that my brothers and I had in store for the family,
friends, and teachers who had the dubious pleasure of
raising us.

Mike is my oldest brother, four years older than
me, and Mark is in the middle, two years older to the day.
When I was five months old Mom divorced our father

and, just seven months later, married our stepdad, Bob, who would go on to adopt us and move the family to his dairy farm. We were cut off from our biological father and wouldn't see him again until much later in life.

Farm life is nonstop. There are no days off and nothing can be done halfway. It's a relentless high-stakes endeavor. Dropping the ball can put your family's livelihood in jeopardy, and might risk the very lives of the cattle upon which everything else depends. After a hard day of farm work—and they're *all* hard days—an older man might want to kick back in his recliner and zone out in front of the tube. I was not an older man. When the working day was done I cut loose hard. This intense cycle of daily work and recreation taught me the meaning of *work hard, play hard,* and I've held true to that motto ever since, for better and for worse.

Playing hard can lead to trouble (as you'll soon see), but there was one thing that could keep my brothers and me out of trouble and that was sports. From the time I could walk we whacked baseballs, shot baskets, wrestled, and played football. I was never a great student; many years later, I realized that I had a form of dyslexia or ADD. If it weren't for sports my school career might have been short and painful. It was sports that pulled me through, gave me a sense of purpose, and helped to lay the foundation for everything that I would eventually become.

But getting good at team sports didn't come without some kicking and screaming. When I was nine years old I would play T-ball with my best friend, Shawn. One day we got called up to play a game in the majors of Little League. This was the big time! I remember that neither one of us did very well. The coach chewed our butts out and told us that we were not ready for the majors. We cried all the way home and, without knowing it, we experienced a miracle: We were motivated. In fact, we were more than that: We were downright angry! *We'll show him,* we said. For the first time that I can remember I let someone's doubt in my abilities fire me up into overdrive. I translated that hurt and humiliation into momentum, energy, and an all-consuming determination to be exactly what he said I could never be. Proving him wrong was a powerful motivator. Maybe I wasn't ready for the majors right that minute, but I sure as hell would be, and I'd make that coach eat his words big time. I rallied Shawn and we set out to become the best two baseball players that we could be. From that day to this one I can still feel the fire that that coach lit with his words, and even now, whenever someone tells me that I can't do something, or that I'm not good enough or smart enough to reach my goals, that fire is rekindled and burns just as hot as it did all those years ago.

Fast forward three years: We're twelve years old, playing in the Little League, working hard, being the best players that we could be, and becoming the stars of the team, just like I knew we could be. The old coach had retired by then, so we never did get to *show him* (unfortunately), but Shawn's dad Kenny was now the coach. And I was perfectly happy with that.

Kenny was like my second dad. He was a great man, I learned a lot from him, but he didn't know much about coaching baseball. That, coupled with the fact that we hailed from the twenty-miles-from-anywhere town of Edison, Washington, ensured that we became the Bad News Bears of our league. True to form, we lost our first game in a blowout. But then an amazing thing happened: Shawn and I, along with some other talented players, pulled the team together and we ran the table for the rest of the year. We went into the championship game against the only team that beat us.

And what a game it was. After pitching three hitless innings, catching three more innings, and going four for four from the plate and driving in two of our five runs, we went on to win the championship for the first time in league history. The championship trophy traveled year to year to whomever won it that year; if a team ever won it three years in a row then the trophy would stay with that team. Although I was now too old to play in Little League, I helped Kenny coach for two more years—and we won the trophy two more times. We were the first team in league history to win the championship three consecutive times, so the Bad News Bears of the county got to keep the championship trophy, a feat that pissed off every other coach. It never felt so good to annoy so many people.

After that first winning year we were the talk of the league and of the little town of Edison. We were celebrated in every corner of our little piece of Washington State and one of those celebrations started me on a path that would challenge me for the rest of my life: One of my teammate's parents let us have a few beers.

By the time I got into seventh grade I was starting on the basketball, wrestling, and flag-football teams. Even though I excelled in sports I still struggled in class. By the end of that school year I was barely passing. After talking with my parents, and giving it some serious thought, I decided to hold myself back and repeat the seventh grade. This is not a decision that you make lightly at that age. It potentially meant ridicule and shame and being separated from my friends. The teachers and school administrators tried to talk me out of it, but it was the right call to make. Above all, it taught me the importance of stepping out of the box and forging my own way, even if it isn't what everyone else is doing. It would have been far easier at the time, believe me, to follow everyone's advice, stay with my peers, and keep struggling, but I knew what was right for me and I made the call. I needed the extra time to get myself where I needed to be and, as hard as the decision was to make, I haven't regretted it for a minute. Even now, while I still value and solicit the advice of my friends and co-workers, at the end of the day I follow my own gut feeling and, aside from a few early missteps (which you'll read about), I've never let myself down. Looking back, I realize what a major positive impact repeating seventh grade made on my life, not only academically, but in learning to chart my own course regardless of the paths that others choose.

My eighth-grade teacher, Mr. Breckenridge, switched classes with the seventh-grade teacher for a couple of periods every day. Mr. B was a big, intimidating man, very strict, and he didn't put up with any bullshit. He raised five boys of his own and he knew exactly how to handle someone like me. He was also the basketball and football coach, so he knew me well, and he knew how to get the best work from me both on and off the field. I never excelled at academics, but he helped me get my grades up to something that was better than just scraping by.

By the time I started eighth grade I was earning decent grades and was not only the star of the basketball and football teams but had become a pretty good wrestler, too. Seventh and eighth graders were allowed to wrestle on the high school freshman team, and on the first day of practice, the coach said that I had gotten fat over the summer. It's true that I had bulked up to one-hundred and seventeen pounds from about a hundred pounds the year before. What can I say; I was a growing boy! My brother Mark told the coach that I just sat around all summer eating peanut butter and jelly sandwiches. *Thanks, Mark.*

15

Once again, someone's dismissive comments burned inside of me, and that whole wrestling season I used that feeling to push myself to an undefeated year. Our team never lost a match. Make me mad and I'll win. That's how I roll.

With the school year over, I spent the summer lifting weights, working out, and spending some quality time getting comfortable with drinking.

Chapter Two

CROSSROADS

As I entered high school, my activities, and everything else happening around me, shot into the fast lane. About the only things that kept me out of trouble were sports, my new girlfriend, and work. For Kenny, I bucked hay bales that weighed about as much as I did. I'd drink and party into the wee hours every night with my friends, only to have Kenny wake me up at the crack of dawn: "Time to load some hay!" Loading the hay was bad enough; doing it with a hangover was agony. Did I learn? I was in high school. Of course I didn't.

One night, Skip and I went to a party in a little town called Bow, about ten miles from home. We grabbed some beer, jumped on Skip's dirt bike, and headed out. We were only fifteen years old, but that never stopped us from partying and riding motorcycles, even on the public roads where getting caught could mean serious trouble. The route to our destination took us along county roads; around multiple ninety-degree turns with big, hazardous drainage ditches on both sides; through the two-block town of Edison past our grade school, the café, the tavern, and the liquor store; to the blink-and-you-miss-it metropolis of Bow, where we finally skidded to a stop and partied until long after dark.

I have no idea how we made the decision, but I was the one who drove us home. Maybe I was the soberest one between us, or maybe I just convinced Skip to let me drive because I liked to be in control. The only thing I know for sure is that neither of us should have been driving: We were fifteen years old, drunk, it was after dark, and we were on a dirt bike on difficult county roads that were dangerous enough under the best of conditions. Somehow, we made the first leg of the trip and blew through Edison without encountering a single vehicle. We had the road to ourselves, but the most dangerous part of the road was just ahead. We rounded the first ninety-degree turn and all was well; we were hauling ass and getting closer to home. As we rounded the second ninety-degree turn I blacked out. We missed a road sign by mere inches, jumped the drainage ditch, and landed next to a telephone pole on the other side.

Skip woke me up, we jumped on the cycle, and finished our homeward journey. The next morning it was business as usual: "Time to load some hay!" There would be no hay loading on this morning, though. We took Skip to the hospital where he was diagnosed with cracked vertebrae. He spent a couple of days there and eventually made a full recovery. I was unscathed.

Again, I didn't learn. But my work ethic was serious and intense, and it helped keep me in line. Also saving me from myself was sports. As a freshman, I was finally able to play my all-time favorite, tackle football. As in every other sport, I was an instant star. I was the team's starting wingback on offence, a defensive back, and the go-to player for returning kickoffs and punts.

At three games into the season we were unbeaten, blowing out all of the other teams. We were the talk of the league. Although I led the team in rushing and total yards, something wasn't right. After every game I was in serious pain and had to go to a chiropractor to get adjusted and have my hips put back where they belonged.

But I played on. Since we were unbeaten, our next game would be on the varsity field, a field upon which no other freshman team had ever played. We faced a team that had won only one game, and there was no way that this one would be their second. We would win; no question about it.

We trailed at halftime. Their running back was exceptional; he ran circles around us and nothing we did could stop him. We had to put an end to it. The coach came to me: "If you lay a big hit on him the team will get fired up and start playing like they should."

This would be a cinch, I thought. As they drove the ball down the field for yet another touchdown, they gave it to their running back and he tore through the line of scrimmage on his way to the end zone. We met head to head at about the three-yard line and he threw me hard on my ass; he was at least fifty pounds heavier than I was and I felt every ounce. The sharp pain in my lower back told me that something was seriously wrong. There was only one thing that could possibly be worse than excruciating pain and potentially permanent injuries, and that would be losing the game. We lost.

Now I was angry. I managed to get showered and changed, but the agony was so intense that I could barely walk from the locker room to the curb where my mom waited to take me to my usual post-game chiropractic session. By the time we got there I was in tears and had to be carried into the office where the chiropractor, after an adjustment, said that most of the pain was in my head and I should be fine.

I missed practice the following week and by game day I could still barely walk, so I stewed on the sideline and watched the team play on without me. Afterward, we went back to the chiropractor and he finally took some x-rays. He had been dead wrong. This time he told me I had a broken back and wanted to put me in a body cast. *And he had said it was all in my head.* Way to go, Doc! My mom and I were fed up with him, so we made an appointment with one of Seattle's top orthopedic doctors who promptly changed my life and broke my heart: I had a degenerative disk disorder, two cracked vertebrae, two deformed vertebrae, and a vertebra that was about a quarter of an inch out of place. I could no longer play sports unless I was willing to risk paralysis.

Most of what had kept me motivated and out of trouble was gone. There was still work, but that wasn't enough for someone with my energy and appetite. I would have to find something else.

Unfortunately, *something else* turned out to be more drinking. My new girlfriend, Julie, and her family, kept me from going completely overboard. One day I told her father, Dennis, about my work on the farm and how much I disliked it. I had already been with Julie for a while and had helped Dennis do some work around their house so he knew that I had a good work ethic and could take direction. Dennis owned a plumbing company called Purves Plumbing with a partner, Steve, and he asked me if I would like to come and work for them instead of hanging out with farm animals. I knew nothing about plumbing, even less about running a business, and the idea of working for my girlfriend's father scared me to death. I said yes. At sixteen years old I got my driver's license, accepted his offer, and started my life in the bold new world of plumbing.

I worked in the warehouse, filled in at the office, delivered parts, whatever they wanted me to do. There would be no smooth sailing, though. Within the first month, while out on a delivery, I got into an accident in "Big Ernie," Steve's gigantic pickup truck. I made a left turn off of the freeway and sideswiped another car, totaling it. No one was hurt, not even "Big Ernie." Not so much as a scratch. Needless to say, Dennis's partner Steve didn't see this as a good sign. To him I was just another cocky sixteen-year-old who thought he had it all figured out. The fact that I was dating his partner's daughter only made things worse.

Steve decided to manipulate me into quitting. The local hospital had a broken sewer line that had been dumping raw sewage under the building for months and someone had to go under there and spread lime all over the mess to kill the bacteria and the smell. Steve handed me the job. What an opportunity! It was the middle of summer and the temperature under the building was over a hundred degrees. Did I mention several months' worth of raw sewage?

The only entrance was through a little hatch in an x-ray lab, and I would have to carry the lime bags through the hatch and into the crawlspace one at a time. And that wasn't even the hard part. I had to wear hip boots, a full set of raingear, rubber gloves, a hood, and a respirator—basically a full hazmat suit—in one-hundred-degree temperatures in a crawlspace filled with human waste. Yes, Steve wanted me to quit. To his astonishment, I not only finished the job, I volunteered to help the plumber repair the line and get everything back to normal. I did it all without one complaint and Steve grudgingly decided that I might be okay after all. He even came to like me and eventually became one of my major mentors. Years later he asked me what I was thinking and why I never complained about the most horrible job imaginable. I told him I took a different approach to it than most people would: Not only did I get paid, I got a hell of workout and weight-loss program at the same time. Besides, there was no way I was going back to the farm, so I figured *a little shit now would mean less shit later.*

But Steve's question made me think about something that hadn't occurred to me before, and it's something that's stuck with me ever since: The way that I handled that one job all those years ago, probably the nastiest job that I will ever have to do, has made all of the difference in my life from that point forward. If I had refused to do it, if I had whined about it, if I had done a half-assed job, it would have confirmed Steve's opinion and possibly changed Dennis's mind about me as well. My entire career in plumbing, which has formed the foundation of everything that I've built, could have some to a screeching halt right there on that day and I would now lead a very different life, and one that probably wouldn't involve becoming a millionaire. I accepted the challenge, put a positive spin on it, and saw the benefits that I could reap from what was otherwise an unpleasant experience.

The key is this: Every decision you make, in one way or another, alters the future course of your entire life. Maybe you just have to decide whether to have a hamburger or a hot dog. Big deal. But maybe you have to choose how to handle a difficult or unpleasant situation in the workplace, or you have to decide whether to accept an opportunity—or a chore—that's been offered to you. I can't tell you which choices to make; you'll have to decide those for yourself, but make those decisions carefully, and know that they may impact your life for decades to come. Choose wisely. If I had made the easy, appealing choice way back then—*I refuse to spend the day in a hazmat suit shoveling shit in a one-hundred-degree crawlspace*—I might have had a more pleasant day and also avoided living a life that is worth writing a book about.

As my junior year began, I was working like a dog, getting by in school, spending time with Julie, and drinking like a rock star. With sports out of the picture, it was up to work and Julie to keep me in line, and I was about to lose one of those: Julie and I broke up, leaving me with only work to mitigate the drinking and partying. It wasn't enough.

The booze and the teenage heartbreak were too much for me to handle and I went into a downward spiral that I couldn't pull out of. At the risk of paralysis, I turned back to sports. Everyone tried to talk me out of it, but I didn't feel like I had a choice. It was either that or booze-soaked oblivion. I needed something intense and all-consuming to keep me out of trouble, and I decided that wrestling would do the trick.

Honestly, wrestling was probably my least-favorite sport, but my injuries meant that football was out of the question. At five-foot-six I wasn't going to the NBA, and I hadn't played baseball since Little League, so wrestling it was. The season was already a few weeks old and they had their starting lineup all locked down. In order to make it onto the varsity team I would have to challenge whomever was starting at my weight classification. Scott was one hundred and thirty-five pounds, a sophomore, and one of the hardest-working kids on the mat. We wrestled, I beat him out for the starting spot, then he challenged me every week trying to win it back. The matches were always close, but he never beat me.

And that season was the end of sports for me; I was done playing on a competitive level. Although I had done well, the risks were too great. I needed to find a way to keep myself under control that didn't threaten to leave me in a wheelchair for the next seventy years of my life. And it would be an uphill battle. I drank heavily most nights, and twice as much on the weekends. But the weekends were made for partying and drinking. Right?

One Saturday night I went with Skip and Ed, another friend, into town to visit some girls and do some partying. We got some beer, as always, and made the twenty-minute trip from Samish Island, in the beautiful San Juan Islands, to Burlington, where our high school was and where most of the people lived. We spent a few hours hitting on girls and guzzling plenty of beer. After exhausting all of the opportunities that the evening offered us, we decided to head back to Samish Island and home.

After making it through all but one of the ninety-degree turns on the route, we crossed onto the island and approached the last hazardous curve, tree lined on both sides, with a sheer cliff on the left behind the trees that dropped a hundred feet straight down to the bay. Skip's house was only a quarter mile ahead. We were almost there.

Ed and Skip had passed out and I, the driver, decided to join them. The car zoomed off the road, snagged a tree at the edge of the cliff, and flipped upside down. We didn't make it home, but at least we weren't in the bay.

Ed finally woke up and shook Skip and me into groggy consciousness. We walked away with nothing more than cuts and bruises. We told our parents that a deer ran out in front of us and, as usual, my mom believed me. Ed's dad, on the other hand, knew better. He said, "Damn, that deer must be getting pretty old by now because I'm sure it's the same one I almost hit when I was in high school."

I clearly needed to find a way to channel my energies that would ensure that I was still around for my high school graduation. The only thing keeping me alive and out of jail was work. I spent every day after school at Purves Plumbing and was determined to learn as much as I could.

Purves was a full-service plumbing company. We did new construction, service, repair, and even had a showroom for retail sales. I worked in every aspect of the company and was determined to learn as much as possible. Steve taught me about estimating and project management, while Dennis showed me purchasing, inventory control, and retail sales. They both taught me the hard facts of running a business.

I became so wrapped up in work and partying that school became an afterthought. Nonetheless, senior year arrived and I had to get through it. The prospect of another months-long academic ordeal was more than I could stand. Something had to be done.

All of my graduation credits were assured except for an English class and a history class. The school had a work program and if you were on target to graduate, and you had a job, you could leave school early to go to work. On the first day of school, Ed and I walked into the office of the vice principal, Mr. Johnson. He liked us in spite of our bad reputations and multiple expulsions. I can't explain it. Maybe he saw a little of himself in us, or maybe he wished he could have as much fun as we did. Either way, Ed closed the door, sat in Mr. Johnson's chair, and put his feet up on the VP's desk. I pulled up a chair next to him and we waited for Mr. Johnson to return.

When he finally showed up he just stood there and shook his head. "What can I do for you gentlemen?" he said. We asked him to have a seat on the student side of his desk, and we got right to the point: We wanted to have free passes all year to come and go to classes as we pleased.

Mr. Johnson knew that I had a full-time job, that Ed was heavily involved in sports, and that we were both on track to graduate. Still, we were surprised when he said, "Sure, boys. But I have a few stipulations. If either of you let your grades fall below passing, your pass will be revoked. Ed, if you miss a practice or a game, your privileges will be revoked. Kelly, if you miss a day of work, your pass will be revoked." We took the deal and got out of that office before Mr. Johnson changed his mind.

I often got paged to work right in the middle of a class. Sometimes, when that happened, I just got up and walked out. If the teacher told me to sit down I said, "Sorry, I'm going to work. Call Mr. Johnson if you have a problem." I worked twenty-four to thirty-two hours a week and even started doing service calls replacing water heaters, toilets, sinks, faucets, or just helping another plumber. I couldn't get enough of it.

School was another subject altogether. There were only two subjects that held my interest—woodshop and friends—and only one of them was educational. Ed and I once fired up a motorbike and rode it into history class. The teacher didn't think this was as funny as Ed and I did, and we both needed to pass that class to graduate. The teacher said, "Why should I give you guys a passing grade? You ordered pizza during class, you tried to tie me up with an extension cord, you haven't turned in a single assignment, and you just rode a motorcycle into my room." That's when the art of negotiation kicked in. We told him he could pass us and never see us again, or he could fail us and have even more fun with us next year. He made the right decision.

Graduation day arrived and they let us participate. We received our diplomas with our class, and then embarked upon one last hurrah before entering into the big bad world of adulthood.

Our class hit the road for Orange County, California. One night out of every year Disneyland would close to the general public so that graduating seniors from across the country could come together to enjoy some good, clean fun at "the happiest place on Earth." That night in Disneyland was indeed good, clean fun. The rest of the trip was one big party.

There were about fifty of us in the group, plus a few guests. The chaperons were Harley, one of our janitors, and his wife. They were two of the sweetest, nicest people, and they were absolutely unprepared to govern a mob of rowdy, hormonal kids. As soon as we arrived at the hotel our beer sensors told us that the convenience store next door sold alcohol. Indeed, there was a great big pyramid of beer sitting right inside the entrance, as if they had built it just to welcome us to Anaheim. We were in heaven.

My brother Mark was living in Thousand Oaks, about an hour and a half away, and he came down to pick up me and a few friends to go up to his place for some partying. We drank beer all the way back to his place, hit a couple clubs, dove into some tequila, and then Mark and I found something to fight about. I have no idea what the disagreement was, but I walked away looking like I'd just been punched out by Mike Tyson.

After a long (and expensive) taxi ride back to Anaheim we found everyone lounging by the pool. Above the pool was a balcony. Someone put two and two together and understood that the trip wouldn't be complete until someone took a dive. As we drunkenly struggled to determine whether or not a diver could clear the concrete and make it into the pool, the people below yelled "DON'T DO IT!" Then from among the crowd I heard, "You can't do it; there's no way you can make it. You'll hit the concrete."

That was all the encouragement I needed. *Can't never did anything,* I thought, and I knew that it was up to me to make this dive happen. I jumped with all my force, head first, and my nose and feet cleared the concrete by scant inches. No one else attempted it. No one else was crazy enough. And seeing my life flash before my eyes calmed me down for the rest of the visit.

By this time I *knew* that I had a drinking problem. It wasn't just partying and the occasional beer. It was serious. But at eighteen years old I was having too much fun and wasn't even close to facing my issues, much less doing something about them. That day was coming, though, and it was coming soon.

Chapter Three

BUSINESS AS USUAL

With high school in the rear-view mirror, I entered the big bad world with exactly one long-term goal in mind: make money and become a millionaire. College wasn't an option for me; even if I did want to go I'm not sure any college would have let me in. My grades were just barely high enough to allow me to pass, and in the absence of sports my chief extracurricular activities, which colleges always seem to be interested in, were drinking and partying. Besides, I was working for Purves Plumbing and would rather make money than sit in a classroom. I had no idea where the plumbing industry would take me, or how my journey would unfold, but I knew how to work and I loved learning about every aspect of the business.

One of my first post-graduation jobs was installing the plumbing at a rest stop outside of town, and we were behind schedule. We all had to work overtime one Saturday to try to get caught up and, of course, Saturday mornings were usually pretty rough for me because Friday night was high-octane party time. Everyone knew I was hungover and there was no way they would cut me any slack. During break I put my head down on a picnic table and fell asleep. Instead of waking me up after the break they put a book of matches under my butt and lit it. *They literally lit a fire under my butt.* I jumped up and got my ass back to work immediately. After all, I wanted to finish the day so I could go party again.

By this time Ed had moved to Phoenix to attend classes at Universal Technical Institute, and along came Doug who knew how to drink and party like I did. Though Doug was in my class we never hung out in school. Once we met at a party and started drinking together trouble wouldn't be far behind, with more drunken episodes and another hair-raising car accident that we all, once again, miraculously survived with barely a scratch.

Even with all the drinking and partying I still learned as much as possible at work. After about a year in the field doing everything from digging ditches, helping on new plumbing jobs, jack hammering until I couldn't feel my arms, doing service work, and crawling under houses, I knew I didn't want to work with the tools forever. Every place I went, I looked around at the wage-earners and tradespeople doing the hard work of building things and keeping them running: the plumbers, the carpenters, the electricians, the people who were really out there in the trenches day after day. Somebody has to do that and I respect the hell out of them. I did it for many years myself, but I couldn't see myself doing it when I was sixty-five years old, especially with old injuries that could flare up at any time. I needed to find a way up that didn't involve college, so I took every opportunity to help out around the office, whether I got paid for it or not, and learn as much as I could. I helped with retail sales, estimating, inventory, anything that needed to be done. Dennis and Steve recognized this and offered me the purchasing job which I gladly accepted.

About this time Ed finished his schooling in Arizona and moved back home. He, I, and another friend decided to rent a place together in town. As you can imagine, our new home became the weekend party place, and if there was no party at our place we went to another or hit the bars. Many mornings we would wake up and look outside to see if our cars were there and then try to figure out who drove home.

One night our roommate got into a fight in the front yard. I was in the kitchen playing drinking games while Ed watched the fight and held everyone back until the other guy started to get the best of our roommate. Ed couldn't have that, so he blindsided the other guy and knocked him down. Then three other guys grabbed Ed and pinned him on the hood of a car. Ed, being his typical smartass self, shouted "I'll give you three seconds to let me up or I'm going to kick all your asses." That's when I was told there was a fight going on out front. I came through the front door as Ed said "ZERO" and flew through the air knocking everyone to the ground. As I stood up one of the other guys gave me another damn black eye.

After calming everyone down and trying to figure out what had happened, Ed grabbed his girlfriend and took off. The rest of us went inside and had peace drinks while we planned what to do to Ed when he returned home. The party broke up and I passed out before he got back.

The following morning, after waking up with a hangover, I walked downstairs to find Ed in the living room watching TV. He asked how I got the black eye and I didn't say a word. Instead, I walked into the kitchen, chugged a glass of water, then came back into the living room and smacked him straight in the face, giving him a matching black eye. Then I went back to bed.

At work, things were going well, or at least they were for *me*. Although I drank and partied at night and on the weekends, when it came time for work I was all in. I was learning more and more each day, but I wasn't yet privy to the company's financials.

Dennis, who owned seventy-five percent of the company, was going through a divorce and wasn't making sound business decisions. Steve knew what was going on and he forced Dennis to buy him out. Six months earlier I had approached Steve and told him I was thinking of moving to Southern California to live with my brother. He talked me out of it, so here I was at a company that he, himself, wound up leaving. I didn't see Steve again for about six months. When we reconnected I discovered that he had a new company and a new partner. And his advice had changed: "Get out of there, kid. That company is a sinking ship and won't be around very long."

So after a lot of sleepless nights I decided to leave all I had ever known, all my lifelong friends and family, and move to southern California. I was twenty-one years old and had never lived outside of the Skagit Valley. This would be a scary move, way out of my comfort zone.

As the big day approached, I said goodbye to all of my family and friends. By this time my brothers and I had reunited with our dad and rekindled our relationship. Mark, unwilling to live with Mom and our stepdad, had tracked him down years earlier and gone to live with him. It was Mark who facilitated the reunion and who took me to meet our dad's third wife and the love of his life until he passed away in 2018. Dad was a very proud man, hardworking, and private. He didn't show his feelings and till the day he died I think he carried bitterness and guilt for losing his boys in the divorce and not being able to see us grow up. I'll never forget the day I said goodbye to him. For the first time he opened up and shared his feelings. It was the only time I saw him cry. His grief over the many lost years taught me a lesson: When I had a family of my own, I would never allow a gulf to develop

between me and my loved ones, no matter how challenging the circumstances may be.

Chapter Four

CALIFORNIA DREAMIN'

Off to southern California I went. I loaded all of my things into a U-Haul and drove south along the coast. Moving in with Mark probably wasn't the smartest decision; he was drinking and partying as much as I was, but he was in the car business and made really good money, especially for a country boy from Washington State. If Mark could do it, I could do it.

I had always been pretty good with money—I seem to have been born with good financial sense, reinforced by watching too many people foolishly throw their money away every pay period—and I had saved some from my time with Purves Plumbing, so I didn't exactly arrive there without a penny to my name. It's a good thing, too: Southern California is seductive, and I spent the first three months or so drinking and sunbathing. I would hang out at Mark's pool until he got off work, then meet him at a bar and drink some more.

One night, after Mark went home, I went to a friend's house and kept drinking. Sometime early in the morning I decided it was finally time to head for home, so I got into my car, drove away, and got pulled over. I ended up in the Ventura County Jail after blowing a .24 alcohol test. It was my first time behind bars. Another milestone!

When Mark picked me up the next morning he was not happy to see me. He told me to get a job or get out. I wanted to sell cars—I liked the money that he was obviously making—but he refused to hire me. So back into the plumbing business I went. I worked for a couple of different companies and my experiences with them made me even more determined to sell cars. Mark's sunny southern California lifestyle had convinced me that the automotive business was the ticket to becoming a millionaire. Despite my pestering, he insisted that I was too shy and quiet (if you can believe it) and that I lacked the qualities necessary for success in sales. According to him, I simply wasn't the "salesman type." But when someone tells me that I can't do something, that's when I get really fired up to prove someone wrong. I talked him into it and he finally gave me a chance.

It was a major learning opportunity. The car business taught me how to deal with people and how to step out of my comfort zone. What you've read so far doesn't paint the picture of a shy and quiet person, but take me away from my circle of friends and *shy and quiet* is what I am. Here's the thing: Shy and quiet people can't succeed at car sales unless they're willing to change. Maybe this is why Mark was reluctant to hire me; if so, he underestimated my determination and my ability to adapt. I was smart enough to understand the qualities that lead to success in auto sales and I was willing to develop them. Most introverted people can't snap their fingers and instantly become extroverted. But we can fake it. I can be the most extroverted person on the planet when the job requires it, and I gave an Oscar-worthy performance. In fact, I was even the top salesman for a few months. I would hit the lot every morning as the most chatty, engaging guy you ever met, and then revert to my natural state at the end of the day. I had learned to change how I came across at the dealership, which was no small accomplishment, but other things were the same as ever:

Drinking and partying were still my top priorities. Ken, who was another salesman at the dealership, also liked to party and drink, so we became good friends (still are to this day) and we eventually moved in together. We worked at the dealership during the day, and hit a bar every night.

We managed the partying and the working pretty well for a while, then it started getting a little out of hand. Despite my typical money-smart ways, we got to the point where we couldn't make rent. Like most Americans, we were living paycheck to paycheck and just getting by. I had never missed a payment on *anything;* even with all of the drinking and partying (which costs money) I was always responsible, but in California my activities had gone to another level. I had to borrow money from my mom just to pay the rent and not become homeless.

Borrowing money from family members went against all of my natural instincts, and I was ashamed to have to ask for it. I placed a high value on independence; come hell or high water I would stand on my own two feet. Unfortunately, hell and high water had come and it was my own damn fault. It should have been a major wake-up call, but instead of looking in the mirror and taking responsibility, Ken and I packed our things and hit the road for Newport Beach and a new job at a different dealership. When we saw the party life at our new home we felt like we had arrived at the Promised Land. This was where we belonged.

Things did not improve. We got jobs, just as we had planned, but I struggled to pay my bills and my drinking affected me at work which, for the most part, hadn't been a problem before. My drinking had always been secondary to my work; now my work was becoming secondary to my drinking. It's a subtle, gradual change, the sort of thing that you might not notice as it's happening, but the shift had occurred.

Things were going from bad to worse when, as if on cue, I got a random phone call from my old boss and mentor, Steve. When I left Washington in 1986, things were pretty dead and there wasn't much construction going on. Now, almost a year later, there was more activity than he and his new partner could handle. Business was booming, the company was growing, and Steve wanted me to come back to Washington and help him run it.

I was twenty-two and living in sunny southern California. The dreary Pacific Northwest was the last place I wanted to be, so I thanked him and politely declined. I was having far too much fun drinking, partying, and chasing girls.

But all was not well in paradise. It was time to get out of the car business; I wasn't doing as well as I thought I should be, and I blamed the dealership for my inability to make enough money to pay my bills. Selling cars was supposed to make me a millionaire! I tried some other sales jobs, the get-rich-quick type, and—surprise!—none of them panned out. Now I was broke. There was only one thing I knew for sure: In the plumbing business I could make ends meet and still have enough left over to support my drinking habit. Even then, though, I didn't like working with tools. At Purves Plumbing I had grown into many other areas of the business; here, where the owners and supervisors didn't know me, I was stuck in the field fixing pipes and unclogging drains. Not my idea of fun. I put my knowledge to work at a retail plumbing business, but it didn't pay as well as working with the tools, so it was back to the tool kits and toilet traps.

Steve called every month, asking me if I was ready to come back and help out, and every time I replied with some variation of, "I'm having too much fun down here, why on Earth would I go back to Washington?" He obviously saw something in me, even if I wasn't yet ready to see it in myself.

As it turned out, circumstances started to narrow my options. One night, one of my friends and I got into a wrestling match in the front yard as we were leaving a party. I don't remember what happened, but I woke up the next morning knowing that something was very wrong. A trip to the hospital revealed the awful truth: I had a broken collar bone.

This was bad news for sure. My arm was in a sling and I literally couldn't afford to miss work. I was working a new condo project in the Laguna Hills area and there was no way I could carry all of my tools up and down ladders all day, not to mention do the actual *work*, with only one arm. Nonetheless, I summoned my usual grit and did the impossible. I had no choice. If I didn't do the work I wouldn't get paid; and if I didn't get paid my troubles would multiply. However bad my present problems may have seemed, having no money would make them all a whole lot smaller by comparison.

I spent the evening in a Newport Beach bar with some friends while I muddled through my predicament. I strolled out to my car to get something and wound up spending the night in the Newport Beach Jail, charged with public intoxication. I wasn't even driving.

Still, Steve continued to call. My life wasn't going anywhere in California. I certainly wasn't getting rich; on the contrary, I was in a downward spiral. I was fed up. I told Steve that I would head north and see what he had to offer.

I hadn't been back to Washington in a couple of years, and I was shocked at what I found. The sleepy little valley I grew up in was booming. The drive-in movie theater and the sprawling strawberry fields that surrounded it were now a shopping mall. The old two-lane road from Burlington to Mount Vernon, strung with fields and fruit stands, was now a four-lane highway with an outlet mall, office blocks, and fast-food joints. Things were going up so fast they couldn't find enough contractors to do the work. If I didn't get the message before, I certainly did now: Steve was overwhelmed and he really did need my help.

I met Steve in his office. He gave me a tour of the facility, walked me through all of his current projects, then took me to his house where we had dinner, polished off a few beers, and talked for hours. I spent a few more days in Washington visiting friends and family before heading back to California where, once again, I thanked Steve and told him that I was staying put. I had reached the point that I was working to support my drinking and partying with nothing left over for the bank. My financial acumen, which I had been so proud of, had gone out the window in favor of booze. I was living paycheck to paycheck, party to party, and even if I wasn't yet ready to admit it to myself, I knew: I was in serious trouble. My confidence was shot, and I refused to believe that I had what it took to do the job that Steve would expect me to do. He still had faith in me, but I didn't have faith in myself.

On the first of December he called me again. To this point he hadn't actually made an offer, he only said that if I helped him out he would take care of me. This time I got the whole story.

Steve and his partner had grown the business from a little two-man plumbing company into three different companies: a plumbing company, a fire-protection company, and an HVAC company. It was a lot of responsibility and it was difficult to manage. Furthermore, because of his partner, Steve felt that he couldn't make me an offer that he thought I deserved. That changed when the pair decided to separate, with Steve keeping the plumbing and HVAC companies and his partner taking the rest.

Once the paperwork was done and everything was divided up, Steve felt he could finally make me an offer that I couldn't refuse. He said, "Here you go kid. I'll give you five percent of the company the day you start. As long as you're here for five years or more, that will be yours. Then you can buy up to forty-nine percent of the company until I retire; then you can buy me out. This is the last call I'm making to you, so think about it, choose wisely, and let me know."

The next couple of weeks, as I made the drive down the 405 freeway onto I-5, turning down Laguna Canyon Road to the jobsite, all I could think about was what I should do. I had a talk with my current boss and told him about the offer that was waiting for me back home. Things were slowing down in California; the company had over a hundred field employees when I started just a year earlier. Now it was down to about twenty-five. He said, "If you do decide to leave, please don't tell anyone else in the company until you're ready to go. If you do, I'll have to lay you off immediately. I'm laying people off left and right, but I want to keep you as long as I can."

That was nice to hear. I didn't know what I wanted, but I did know what I *didn't* want. I didn't want to be working with the tools and in the field for the rest of my life. I made my decision.

I told Steve that I'd be back in January and ready to go to work. I broke the news to my boss the next morning. He congratulated me and said that I could go ahead and take off; I didn't need to finish the day.

I left the jobsite and turned onto Laguna Canyon Road toward the picturesque Pacific Coast Highway back to Newport Beach. I had no idea what awaited me, but I did know that it was time to say goodbye to California. I had been given the opportunity of a lifetime. Now it was all up to me.

Chapter Five

SICK AND TIRED

My old buddy Skip flew down to California to make the trek back to Washington with me. We loaded my clothes into my '72 Chevelle and made the eighteen-hour drive in as much of a straight shot as we could manage, only stopping for food, gas, and a few car difficulties.

Since I only had three hundred dollars to my name, owed five hundred on my car, and was a full-blown alcoholic, I moved back in with my mom and her third husband, Gary, until I could afford to get a place of my own.

On January 22^{nd,} 1990 the next chapter of my life began as I started working at Steve's company,

Commercial Plumbing, Inc., which was mainly a new-construction plumbing company doing light commercial work and residential jobs on custom homes. I started by doing all of the purchasing, the residential estimating, the scheduling, and anything else that needed to be done around the office and warehouse. When I wasn't at work I slipped right back into my nightly pattern of drinking and partying.

One evening, after settling in for a couple of months, I went out to a bar with some friends. When it was time to leave, they decided to make me the designated driver. Big mistake. We got back to my buddy's house where I planned to stay the night, but I couldn't just pull into the driveway and park the car. Nope, I decided to do a few donuts right there in the middle of the road. I had a great time, and so did the police officer across the street who took me directly to jail.

After being processed I refused all sobriety tests, a decision that I don't recommend repeating. My buddy bailed me out, and we went back to his place where I spent the night before heading back to my mom's the next day. I spent two days in bed with a hangover, thinking the events of the night before were all a dream. When I finally got up and started getting ready for work, I opened my wallet and pulled out the ticket. Nope, not a dream.

That moment, with that piece of paper in my hand, changed my life forever. I was sick and tired of being sick and tired. I was drinking and partying nonstop. At the end of the day I felt horrible and it took a terrible toll on my life. How much better would I be at my job, with money, with girls—with *everything*—if I didn't put such a priority on booze and parties? I didn't want to continue what I was doing; the hangovers had become agonizing; I couldn't bear them. I didn't want to live like this for one more day. Besides, I knew if I didn't do something I was going to end up dead or behind bars. And I didn't even want to think about the fact that I could wind up killing someone *else*. I had to change.

Everyone has a different rock bottom, and that weekend was mine. I had always dreamed of being rich, and I had finally come to a point in my life that it was time to grow up and go after my dreams instead of drinking and partying my life away.

I went to work that morning knowing that the first thing I had to do was explain to Steve that I got a DUI. Did I just blow the opportunity of a lifetime? I walked into his office and he was right there waiting for me. How was my weekend? I told him the bad news and showed him my ticket. For the first time in my life I admitted that I was an alcoholic and needed help. Steve had become a mentor to me, my greatest friend, and a father figure. He wasn't angry. He didn't judge. He said, "Don't worry kid, you'll get through this."

I didn't know what to do or where to go; I didn't know the first step to take, but I thought that my brother Mark would be a good place to start. He had gone through treatment himself just a year earlier, and he suggested that I do the same as soon as possible. That day I called a local treatment facility; twenty-four hours later I arrived at 121 South Spruce Street in Burlington for an evaluation and walked out with a plan for treatment.

I attended an outpatient program once a week for six months. It wasn't easy, but what I had been doing to myself and my body had been far worse. My tolerance for alcohol was rapidly declining, and everything that I read and learned told me that diminishing alcohol tolerance is a sign of impending liver failure. I was twenty-four. That alone was enough to scare the hell out of me. Combine it with all the stupid shit I did when I was drinking and there is no doubt that I had been on the path of self-destruction.

I have what psychologists call an addictive personality. Aside from constantly seeking a bigger thrill, one of the traits is unbridled enthusiasm: When I like something I jump straight down the rabbit hole. I am all in. For years alcohol had been my focus and it came with a whole host of troubles. Now, with help from the treatment facility, I had to face it head-on and shift my enthusiasm into other, more productive directions. I learned that the same energy that fueled my alcoholism could be channeled into fitness, work, academics, you name it. I could direct it anywhere I liked; I just had to harness it. In the coming years I would do just that.

But right now I was still coming to terms with my condition and one of the hardest parts of that was telling all of my friends and family that I was an alcoholic. At least I could tell them that I was dealing with it and heading in the right direction, but it was still excruciating. I had already told Mark, who had been telling me for the past year that I needed to quit, so breaking the news to him was actually a relief.

Telling my mom was another story. I had to tell her that I wasn't the person she thought I was, and that I had let her—and everyone else in the family—down. Although we had drunk together, and she knew about some of the stupid shit I had done, it broke her heart to learn that her Golden Child was an alcoholic. In fact, she almost tried to talk me out of admitting it. She had to accept that not only was one of her sons an alcoholic, *two* of them were. She eventually found that all three of her boys were afflicted when our oldest brother Mike broke the news to her two years later. But she was there for me, as she had always been, and her love and support never wavered.

Dad was next. As I said earlier, he was a man of few words, and he wasn't very sympathetic. When he found out he said, "I'm glad you pulled your head out of your ass before you killed someone or yourself." If you ever want to know what tough love is, I think my dad invented it. He was a no-bullshit guy and he told it the way it was. Although he didn't raise me, he is in my blood, and his simple, direct manner has helped me in life and business.

Finally, I had to tell my friends. If you ever want to find out who your real friends are, tell them you're an alcoholic and need their support. Ed, who had been my biggest drinking and partying buddy, was shocked until I explained a few things to him. Did he ever notice that, when we lived together, there was never any beer left in the fridge from the night before? Or how many times he had to take care of me when I blacked out? After realizing what I had done, and what I had become, and that I was finally taking ownership of it, he became one of my biggest supporters.

When Ed and I first started hanging out in high school, Mom didn't like it. She even told me I shouldn't hang out with him. There was always trouble when Ed and I were together, and most people seemed to think that Ed was a bad influence on me. What a shock to realize and accept that I was the one who had been the bad influence.

Another friend of mine, Kevin, became one of my biggest supporters even though we had never done the drinking and partying that Ed and I had done. Ed, Kevin, and I have stayed very close friends, always challenging each other and pushing ourselves to our limits in every good and positive way. Thank God they were there for me in those early days of becoming sober. They could see the man that I *could* be, and they helped me get there. I couldn't have done it without them.

One evening, while I was out with the guys, a girl who I had seen a few times approached us with the obvious intention of getting my friend's attention. She led him back to her own group of friends and, seeing as we were guys and they were girls, the rest of us followed. We all introduced ourselves, did our best to be smooth, and started chatting each other up. One of them attracted my attention more than the others and before long we were focused squarely on one another. Her name was Heather. I had known about her since high school, she had even dated my brother Mark once (once!), but she was two years ahead of me and had been out of my league. During all of that time I had never done more than say hello to her. Now, with high school a thing of the past, those two years of seniority were meaningless. The playing field was level and I had the ball. She was beautiful and hot, more than enough to grab my attention. I was floored, but not by her looks. She was together. She had it all figured out. She had a great career in medical records and, at twenty-five-years old, she already owned her own home while her peers were renting apartments, living with their parents, or still going to school. Her life was going nowhere but up. On top of all of this, she was the sweetest person I had ever met. As a woman, she was enchanting. More than that, she represented everything that I wanted to be: successful, stable, secure, confident, and moving in the right direction. Of all of the opportunities that I had been offered, of all of the chances that I had been given, I was determined to seize this one above all others. I needed to see her again, and I had to show her the best version of myself that I could be, but no matter how well we got along that evening, convincing her to go out with me again, just the two of us, took some work. The Schols didn't have a great reputation in the valley, and she had already had a taste of us when she dated Mark (remember: Once!). Thankfully, and without my knowledge, her friends talked her into giving me a three-date audition. I must have passed; those first three dates turned into a two-year courtship. I loved her, I treasured every moment that we spent together, and she made me a better man.

But, at the time, I hadn't exactly left the past behind me. I still had to face the fact that I had a DUI and cope with the impact that it would have on my future. As I said, I had refused the breathalyzer and all other testing at the police station after being arrested. In Washington State at that time, if you refused any test your driver's license was automatically suspended until your court date. I immediately hired an attorney who appealed my case so I could drive on a temporary license until my trial date. It's a good thing, too, because my court date wouldn't come around for about a year.

Refusal to take the tests brought even more problems. It meant that I was automatically considered guilty, and since we appealed it to get a temporary license I would have to go in front of the superior court to prove my innocence. I knew I *wasn't* innocent, but I thought maybe I could get the ticket reduced or deferred. As my attorney was preparing me for court he asked if I would like a jury trial or have the judge decide the case.

By now I had been sober for about a year and my life was turning around. I moved out of my mom's house and was living in a small one-bedroom apartment close to work where I spent my time reading about alcoholism, going to counseling, going to work, and spending time with Heather.

Our community was one where everyone knew everyone else, or at least knew someone who did. It was tight-knit in good ways and bad. So when my attorney asked me which kind of trial I wanted I asked if we had any chance of choosing the judge. One of the superior court judges was a longtime friend of the family, Gil Mullen, a towering, intimidating man, and respected in the community for his years of service as a deputy sheriff, attorney, and now superior court judge. If he could do the trial then maybe I would have a shot at a reduced sentence. I thought it sounded like a great idea, but my attorney said that we wouldn't know who the judge would be until we got there. So much for that.

I was also advised to get involved in some community organizations as a way of demonstrating how I was changing my ways and attempting to atone for my past behavior. As with so many other things, I threw myself into this new arena with gusto. I joined the chamber of commerce, the Rotary, and the Economic Development Alliance of Skagit County and helped out with their local fundraisers. All of the turmoil surrounding my DUI case had one positive, lasting effect: It got me involved in the larger community in ways I hadn't been before and it made me appreciate in a very real way what those organizations and the dedicated people behind them were doing every single day. It made me see the good that I could do by investing in something that was larger than myself, and it's a lesson I've never forgotten.

As we met in my attorney's office the morning of the trial, he briefed me on how the day would go. The arresting officers would take the stand one at a time and answer questions from the DA. Then my attorney would cross-examine them. Then we'd take a recess, after which

I would get on the stand to be questioned and cross-examined. It all sounded just like a TV show.

We walked into the courtroom and there sat Mr. Mullen. I was ecstatic. But then the realization of the court system, and seeing Mr. Mullen in his element, scared the ever-living hell out of me. The seriousness of my situation came down on me hard. As I sat there sweating to death like I had just run a marathon (complete with elevated heart rate), the court proceedings began. I don't think I heard a word the officers, the DA, or my attorney said. So many things were running through my head. My fate, for the rest of my life, might be decided right here, today, in this courtroom, and it wasn't fun. Before I knew it we were on recess. My attorney and I went into the hallway and he briefed me again. Was I ready to take the stand? I was far from ready. I thought I was going to be sick right there.

Then the recess was over and we were back in the courtroom. Mr. Mullen asked if there was anything either side would like to say before the proceedings continued. My attorney stood and asked for the case to be dismissed on a paperwork technicality. Mr. Mullen leafed through the documents and did something that I never expected to see. He scolded the officers, telling them that, when he was a deputy, someone got away with murder due to a paperwork technicality and that he, himself, had made the error. It was a lesson he wouldn't forget and he wanted to make sure that the officers in his courtroom learned it, too. He banged his gavel and dismissed the case. I'm not sure who was more shocked, me or the DA who yelled indignantly at Mr. Mullen: "You can't do that! He's guilty!" Mr. Mullen very firmly said, "Ma'am, I am the superior court judge and I am following the law, unlike your officers. This case is dismissed."

All I could think about was my incredible luck. Years later I found out that the work I had done in turning my life around had made a big impact on Mr. Mullen. Steve, and maybe a few other people, had been in contact with my attorney about the changes I made in my life, and how I had gotten involved in the community. Like I said, it was a tight-knit town. I am thankful for the break I got that day, and I also learned something that has made a huge difference in my life ever since: If you want good things to happen it's up to you to make the changes so that good things *can* happen.

As of the writing of this book I have been sober for twenty-nine years and counting, but the challenges didn't stop when I decided to change my life, they just took different forms.

Chapter Six

MILLIONAIRE IN THE MAKING

Steve believed in me, stood behind me, and became the kind of mentor that most people only dream about, not only in business, but in life, in finances, in pretty much any area where a twenty-four-year-old guy could use some advice and guidance. Steve was there. He knew that I dreamed of being a millionaire, that I had the drive to make it happen, and he freely shared his wisdom. As irresponsible as I had been in many areas of my life, with the exception of my time in California, which was a definite wake-up call, I had always been good with money. Now Steve helped me take that to another level. When I lived in California there was a strong competitive-spending culture as everyone around me tried to outdo one another to have the fanciest cars, the finest clothes, the priciest shoes. It's a financially self-destructive way to live and I knew it; my own inborn fiscal compass served me well. Now Steve was about to give me my first real dose of dollars-and-cents book smarts: He threw a paperback on my lap and said, "Read this, kid."

Are you serious? I don't think I'd read a whole book in my life, and I wasn't exactly excited about starting one now. What good could it possibly do me? I looked at the cover. *The Millionaire Next Door: The Surprising Secrets of America's Wealthy,* by Thomas J. Stanley and William D. Danko. Well, I did want to be a millionaire, so maybe this book would be worth the effort.

I was hooked immediately. *The Millionaire Next Door* resonated with me like nothing I'd ever experienced. One of the book's key points is that there are millionaires right on the street where you live. We don't recognize them because they don't live the lifestyles that we've come to associate with the wealthy. They don't drive Rolls-Royces or have private aircraft. They don't live in palaces or have armies of servants. Most wealthy people live modestly, driving ten-year-old cars, living in middle-class homes in the suburbs, and shopping at Walmart. Their frugal, no-frills lifestyles are one of the key reasons that they are millionaires. They understand that money can be saved, invested, and put to better uses than spending it on expensive homes, fancy cars, and exotic vacations that make them *look* wealthy while depleting their bank accounts.

Reading *The Millionaire Next Door* helped me to crystallize my own ideas about money and how to manage it. What were once vague ideas swimming around in my head were now a philosophy, and this new understanding helped me grasp how I fell off of the financial wagon in California, and to ensure that it wouldn't happen again. Best of all, Steve basically *was* the millionaire next door so it was easy to discuss the book with him, learn how he had applied its principles to his own life, and how I could apply them to mine.

As my financial future began to come into focus, a few other things started to move into place. After work on June 10th 1992, I went to Heather's house where she was making my birthday dinner. I had gotten sick and was exhausted from the workday, but birthdays and holidays were big deals to her so I went anyway. We had talked about marriage and she was pretty anxious about wanting to move forward. In fact, she had said that there was no point in staying together if I couldn't see us married. Like many guys, I thought of marriage with a combination of joy and dread. I loved Heather and treasured the idea of spending my life with her, yet marriage seemed so... *permanent*. But wasn't I spending all of my free time with her anyway? As we sat on her couch talking, I decided to override my reluctance and do what I knew I really wanted to do in spite of any lingering misgivings: I popped the question. I wasn't sure that I was ready, and Heather wasn't sure that I was serious, but when she realized I was, she accepted.

We planned the wedding for August 28th, which gave us less than three months to plan everything. When the day came, we were married by the honorable Mr. Mullen, who was far happier to see me this time than he was when I was a defendant in his courtroom. I can't recall who decided to plan the wedding on such an accelerated timetable. Was Heather worried that I would chicken out, or was I worried that I would get cold feet? I don't remember, but I *do* remember my friend driving me to the wedding and pulling over because I thought I was going to be sick.

Heather and I spent the next few years working, remodeling an old farmhouse that we'd bought, and settling into married life. In 1994 we welcomed our first daughter into the world, and in 1997 our second daughter arrived. Our family was complete. We spent time with our friends and their kids doing all of the fun family things like camping, watersports, birthdays, barbeques, and lawnmower racing. Yes, you read that right: A group of friends and I suped up a few riding mowers and raced them at county fairs and other events for some good old-fashioned redneck fun!

But it wasn't all fun and games. We were both working crazy hours, sometimes crossing paths during the day so one of us could watch the kids while the other one went to work. I also worked plenty of weekends and took the girls to the office if Heather had other things going on so that we wouldn't have to pay for daycare. We avoided eating out, didn't buy things we didn't need, and kept our entertainment options cheap and close to home.

When we got married, we set goals and agreed that we would do whatever we had to do to eventually buy out Steve and take ownership of Commercial Plumbing. All of our friends were either building or buying newer and bigger homes, and we had started designing Heather's dream house, but we both knew it would have to wait. If we sacrificed in the short-term, the long-term gains would be incredible. Instead of building our house we bought as much Commercial Plumbing stock as we could afford, knowing that it was the key to our financial future. Ownership of the company was the light at the end of the tunnel, and the bedrock upon which we would build everything that followed.

At last, the day came: Steve announced that he would retire on March 31^{st,} 2002—Good Friday. My first day of ownership would be April Fool's Day. I'm not sure who the joke was on, but it was less than a year after the September 11th attacks and the economy was in the toilet. We would have our work cut out for us.

Steve had a son named Michael, whom we called "Oly," whose life had been a pretty big mess. He had worked for the company on and off for ages, but Steve never thought about him running the company or even being a part owner until the last couple of years before he retired. In that time, Oly had done a fantastic job of turning his life around and had transformed himself into one of our top journeyman plumbers. Steve asked if I would be willing to have Oly as a partner moving forward. I hadn't purchased all of the stock yet, and with the way the economy was going I would have a tough time buying it all before Steve retired. Steve knew this and he proposed gifting Oly twenty-five percent with the condition that Oly had to stay employed with me for at least five years, or the stock would revert back to Steve and I could buy it from him. I agreed and on April Fool's Day 2002 I became the majority owner of a multimillion-dollar company with no idea what the economy—or I—was going to do.

Also in 2002 I faced death for the very first time. My stepdad Bob, who raised me and my brothers, came down with lung cancer. This was a man who took on three rowdy boys when we were all toddlers and was there for us in good times and bad. He taught us the meaning of hard work and the importance of having respect for others. After fighting for a year and a half, and being by his side for every step of the journey, I came to realize that death is a part of life and we will all have to face it. Some people look at death as something that's too difficult or painful to confront, but going through it with Bob made me look at in a different way and be able to talk about it.

That's when I turned to my brother Mark. He was still in the car business and had become very successful. The pressure of growing a company during difficult times, with the full knowledge that a small army of employees counted on me to take care of them and their families, was enormous. I needed help. Mark told me that if I worked on myself as a person and as a leader, everything else would fall into place. One of the things that had made him such a phenomenal salesman was a cassette-and-workbook series by Brian Tracy called *The Universal Laws of Success and Achievement,* a holistic self-improvement system that touched on every aspect of life, including finances, relationships, attitude, communication, even health and wellness. Thanks to Mark and Mr. Tracy, my pickup became a university on wheels, and what used to be wasted downtime while I drove between sites became some of the most valuable hours of the day.

My dedication and new self-improvement regimen paid dividends and, over the next few years, things could not have been better. The company was growing and we were making good money. We finally started building Heather's dream house in 2002, the year that I took over the company, moved into it in October 2003, and paid it off in June 2006. For most homeowners, paying off your mortgage seems like a goal that is impossibly far in the future. Heather and I were astonished that we were able to do it so quickly, in record-setting time. The day we made our final payment was like a holiday. "Wow, we did it!" There's no other feeling quite like it.

Except maybe this one: I had been so focused on growing the company and building our assets that I had failed to take stock of our net worth. When I did, it was over 1.4 million dollars. It was breathtaking. It was also sobering and humbling to realize that, through the simple application of hard work, teachability, frugality, sacrifice, and seizing every opportunity, I had achieved my lifelong goal of becoming a millionaire—and it had happened without me even realizing it. I had always imagined watching my accounts grow until I reached the finish line: Yay, I'm a millionaire! But it wasn't like that at all. We reached it, surpassed it, and kept chugging along, eyes still fixed to the goal. And I wouldn't have had it any other way.

Oly and his wife also paid their house off in just a few short years, then we brought in another partner, Brad, and he and his wife paid off their home as well. We built a culture of mutual support that encouraged everyone to succeed. A rising tide lifts all boats.

Brad was hired the day that Heather and I were in the hospital waiting for the arrival of our oldest daughter.

We had been looking for a warehouse person and Brad had come in for an interview. Steve, who never did anything half-assed, called to tell me he may have found someone for the warehouse position and he wanted to ask me what I thought of him. I asked, "Does this guy know anything about plumbing or running a warehouse?" Steve, who was way into golf at the time, would only say that Brad was a scratch golfer and a clean-cut young man. I said, "That's great, Steve, *but does he know anything about plumbing or running a warehouse?*" Again, I was told that he's a scratch golfer. With my patience running short, and Heather about to deliver, I said, "Okay, go ahead and hire him; I have to go." Needless to say, Brad was a great hire and now he's one of my partners with the same mindset that Oly and I have.

Heather and I were truly living the American Dream. We bought a travel trailer, a ski boat, a golf cart, and, with another couple, a vacation condo in Crescent Bar, Washington. We paid cash for it all. Things were going well for our family and Commercial Plumbing, and Heather was now the owner of a medical-records copying business that she and her mother had started years earlier. We felt pretty secure in our position, enough so that we decided to take care of a nagging issue that had bothered me ever since I took over Commercial Plumbing: We didn't own the company's building or the land beneath it. Steve had kept those, but as the majority owner I thought they should belong to me. Since things were going so well, Heather and I negotiated with Steve to buy the structures and the real estate, and he agreed to sell. In June of 2007, after writing a 1.2 million dollar contract, everything was ours. Now, for the first time, it seemed like all of the game pieces were on my side of the board and I looked forward to the limitless horizon of tomorrow. What could possibly go wrong?

Chapter Seven

THE TIDE GOES OUT

By the summer of 2008, Commercial Plumbing was so busy that we could name our own prices on jobs. For many businesses, this is a holy grail. Most of our work— eighty-five percent—was new construction, and sixty-five percent of *that* was residential: custom homes, high-end tract homes, and condos.

Prices on these properties had become ridiculously expensive. Brad's wife Kris, who worked at the bank, told him about some of the loans they were writing and how people were buying homes they really couldn't afford. Our accounts receivable (the amount of money that clients owed to the company for services rendered) was over a million dollars. When we looked at all of these things together—incredibly expensive homes, buyers overextending themselves, banks writing crazy loans—we realized that things were starting to look dicey. If people were building houses that they couldn't afford, and these same people owed us over a million dollars... well, you can see why we were worried. We had over forty employees and were doing close to six million dollars in annual sales with double-digit net profit. Normally this would be outstanding, but we had the nagging feeling that the real estate and home-construction bubble would burst, and soon. We called a management meeting to figure out what we could do to stay ahead of what we saw as a serious looming problem. Our solution was to rebrand ourselves as CPI Plumbing and Heating, reorient our efforts toward service/repair and light commercial work, and get out of residential new construction, which was the most competitive market in our industry. This helped to insulate us against downturns, since the majority of our work up until then had been in residential new construction. If the bubble did burst, we didn't want to be a part of it.

As part of this process we joined a best-practice group called Service Roundtable which provided a nationwide chat forum for HVAC, plumbing, and electrical contractors to share their advice and experience. I read chats from all over the country about construction projects being put on hold and people losing their houses. Then it happened: The economy crashed. We dodged the bullet thanks to our proactive restructuring and the fact that the Pacific Northwest is always a little slower than the rest of the country when it comes to ripples (or tidal waves) in the real estate and construction markets.

As the rest of the economy went south in 2009, CPI had its biggest year ever, but we knew it wouldn't last. At this time we were a union company, and all of the plumbers and apprentices were part of the local union. We had joined them years earlier so that our employees would have the benefits that came with union membership, and to make it easier for us to source labor (the stronger the economy is the harder it is to find workers). The union contract expired at the end of May 2009 but the employees continued working pending adoption of a new one. During our contract negotiations with the union, the contractors offered a fair and substantial raise to the employees, but they turned it down.

By now it was the first of August 2009 and there was no end in sight. The union business administrator had told all of the contractors that when the contract did settle CPI would have to pay retro wages back to June 1st. CPI was still busy; we had quite a few contracts for jobs, and things hadn't started collapsing in the Pacific Northwest yet, but the writing was on the wall: We weren't getting jobs like we used to. The tsunami was indeed coming, and paying all of those back wages could be a problem. We had already shifted to more of a service/repair and light commercial model, so we decided to take the next step and drop out of the union. I wrote to the union business administrator explaining that I couldn't run my business without knowing what my costs were going to be because they wouldn't settle the contract. I had a meeting the next morning and told all of the employees that, come Monday, we would be a non-union company. If they wanted to stay, they could show up Monday morning as usual and fill out a new application; otherwise, they were welcome to report to the union hall.

By August of 2010 we had gone from doing six million dollars a year to barely three million. Then, on August 10th, I received a notice from the Washington State Union Pension Plan that was like a punch in the face: CPI owed them $396,000 because we had dropped out of the union pension plan. We had three years to pay it, and they would start taking quarterly payments of $34,000 even if they had to seize it from our accounts. There was no way that we could afford this. I hired an attorney to see what our options were, but things were about to get worse. About a month later we got another letter, this one from the National Pension Plan. We owed *them* $148,000 and would have to pay it within three years as well.

These letters could have spelled the death of our company and the end of everything that we had worked so hard to achieve. After a lot of emotions, anger, frustration, and pain we entered into negotiations with the union to settle the fines. The national pension would settle for a lesser amount, which pretty much covered our attorney fees. The Washington pension, on the other hand, would not. Their position was both harsh and firm: Pay in full or go out of business.

We were at the end of our rope, not knowing what to do or how to come up with the money. With nowhere else to turn, I decided to go back to what had worked for me before: doing what I could to improve myself, just as I had when I bought the company.

I dove back into *The Universal Laws of Success and Achievement* and went to my first-ever Service Roundtable conference in Las Vegas. The keynote speaker was Kenny Chapman who called himself the Blue Collar Coach. His speech hit me hard. His life had been similar to mine when I was young. I saw myself in him, and instantly knew that he could help me get through one of the most challenging situations I had ever encountered. I bought his book, *The Six Dimensions of C.H.A.N.G.E.,* and spoke with him for a few moments after his address. He told me about a new program that Service Roundtable was rolling out called *Service Nation Alliance,* a group of contractors from across the country that would meet once a week on a conference call to discuss business practices and share advice. Kenny would lead the group, so for me it was a no-brainer. I wanted to improve as a business owner, leader, father, husband, and friend and Kenny's messages were more about personal development than business. Kenny's message was just what I needed.

When I returned to CPI, we called a planning and strategy meeting to figure out how we could pay off the union without crippling our business. We put together a plan that included cutting wages, lowering overhead, and tightening our focus even more on service and repair. It was painful, but it worked. The service department grew, and we were able to make the payments to the union. The company was stable, and I was in the clear—for now.

Chapter Eight

FOR BETTER OR FOR WORSE

Everything seemed to be going well at work and with the kids, but It seemed like Heather and I were growing apart. We had a great relationship, but we were slowly coming to realize that we were more of a business partnership than a couple. Everything revolved around our kids, our work, and our friends—all of which were important—but nothing revolved around us. The day-to-day activities of life took over and we didn't take the steps that we should have to strengthen and fortify our marriage. We focused on accomplishing our goals and raising the kids, and everything we had set out to do we had done. CPI was stable, and her business was doing really well. As a business partnership, we were successful and prosperous.

The girls were in high school and we were making plans for them to go to college. Our daughters were beautiful and smart, but their parents had very different child-raising philosophies, and it was a major source of friction in our marriage. Heather grew up in a household where punishment was a rarity; her parents loved and adored their children but allowed them to do as they pleased. I, on the other hand, was raised with an iron fist, to never talk back (which I of course did, earning me several ass-kickings), to be hard-working and self-sufficient. As a couple, Heather and I applied our respective upbringings to our own children, bringing the best of both upbringings together, soft and inclusive, yet disciplined and structured. When the girls made a mess, she did what most mothers with a huge heart would do and cleaned it up for them; if they refused, Heather would clean it up for them. I, on the other hand, would throw the mess in a garbage bag and put it out for the trash. It sometimes broke my heart, but we taught them both compassion and tough love.

If the girls smarted off, or were otherwise disrespectful to me or Heather, I was the one who punished them. This would break Heather's heart and sometimes she would get upset with me for being too tough. Like a lot of couples, I thought she was sometimes too sweet, which is why I fell in love with her in the first place. And she thought I was too demanding. I didn't like being the one who doled out all of the behavior-modification, but I felt that the girls needed both. If they only knew how it tore at my heart to be the disciplinarian. They are thriving in the real world today because of the guiding hands of their parents when they were young.

I was the driving force and disciplinarian in our family, while Heather was the peacemaker; more than that, actually: She let them be themselves and waited on them hand-and-foot. She would do anything to allow them to express themselves freely and enjoy being young; she was everybody's best friend and put everyone else—especially our daughters—ahead of herself. Her reluctance to impose any limits on them frustrated me at times, but my brother pointed out that, between the two of us, we had raised two amazing daughters. We definitely had differing parenting styles; I think that's how God intended it to be. We seemed to be on the same page with everything else. At least, I thought we were.

One day, while discussing the girls' upcoming college careers, I pointed out that we had nearly reached our goal of paying off the CPI building that we had bought from Steve. What should our next round of goals be?

I have always been goal-oriented. Goals sustain me, they motivate me, and they keep me plowing ahead when things get tough. For as long as I could remember, going all the way back to grade school, I had always been aiming at a target. No one taught me to be this way; it was bred into me and it is inseparable from who I am. If I hadn't had goals, and the drive to achieve them, I would still be down on the farm throwing hay bales or working with the tools for someone else. Goals are essential.

It hadn't occurred to me that Heather might not have the same thirst to always be reaching for more. She got upset and asked me if I could ever be satisfied with what we had, if I could ever stop pushing for the next thing that was just out of reach. I thought about it for a minute and said, no, I would *never* be satisfied. I could be grateful, but I would never be satisfied. I asked her if *she* was satisfied. Yes, she said, she was. "I have everything I could have asked for in my life. I have a great business with great employees, my dream home, wonderful kids, the best friends anyone could ask for, and a great husband." Wow. Sometimes I wish I weren't made this way, where enough is never enough, and could be more like her, living in the moment, enjoying life's blessings, and feeling content right where I am.

It was at that moment that I knew we really *weren't* on the same page. We needed help.

Years earlier, when I began my personal-development program, my brother warned me that if we didn't embark on this journey together then we would eventually grow apart. We had been married for nineteen years and seeing both of my parents married three times each and both of my brothers go through divorces, I was determined to make things work. I was already trying to improve as a leader of CPI so that we could get through the union liability, but now it was time to work on myself as a husband and a father. In order to make this work, though, it couldn't be a solo project. Heather had to be in on it. We talked about marriage counseling, but Heather insisted that I was the one who needed counseling, especially since I was so strict with the girls. Thankfully, to save our marriage (and to appease me) she eventually came around and we started seeing a counselor together.

That same year I started reading books on how to parent teenage girls. Also, the girls and I took a couple of vacations without Heather, who said she was too busy at work to take the time off. She had never missed a family vacation before, and I doubt that she wanted to miss these. She had always looked forward to them and enjoyed them. I think she wanted to help me tighten my bond with our daughters and thought that her staying home would help. Like I said, she put everyone else ahead of herself.

Heather's father passed away in May of 2012. Her mother had passed ten years earlier. Her mother's death had taken an enormous toll on her, and her father's death was no different. That summer, the girls and I took trips to our condo in Crescent Bar without Heather. She had always come with us before. Again she claimed she was too busy at work, along with all of the volunteer work she was doing. I think she was trying to bury her grief in work, but all the stress only seemed to make things worse. It got so bad that, by the first of August, she was having panic attacks that caused heart palpitations. Of course she wouldn't tell me or the girls; she didn't want us to worry about her, but one day, while she was driving, it got so bad that she almost passed out. Instead of calling me or going to the doctor, she called my buddy Kevin, a pharmacist. He sent her directly to a walk-in clinic where they did an EKG. They told her that yes, she was having heart palpitations, but they weren't life-threating.

At this point Heather's secret was out. Another friend, a cardiologist, immediately ordered a nuclear stress test and an echocardiogram, which confirmed what we already knew: She was having non-life-threatening heart palpitations. While I thought they might be stress-induced, there was no medical agreement. No one knew for sure what was causing them.

We celebrated our twentieth anniversary on August 28th 2012, and on Labor Day weekend we went on a camping trip with about fifteen other families as we wrapped up the summer before getting the girls ready for another year of high school. Our oldest daughter was entering her senior year and would then be off to college; our youngest was starting her sophomore year. It was a wonderful weekend, everyone enjoyed each other's company and friendship. It was a great way to end the season.

We were also solidifying our daughters' future college plans. Society tells us that a college education is a necessary ingredient of a successful life, yet I built a remarkably successful life without one. Most people assume that I have a degree and they're surprised when I tell them I don't. My own daughters friends didn't know until they were well into high school. You don't need a degree to be successful, but without one you'll need plenty of grit, determination, skill, drive, and an understanding of how to apply what you know. And don't expect the Fortune 500 companies to hire you if you don't have a degree. If you want to get ahead you'll have to start your own business or apprentice into a position in someone else's.

Aside from the obvious value of a college degree in corporate America, what is a formal education worth? I don't think that anything is worth more than a great work ethic, life experiences, common sense, and the *endless desire to learn something new.* I have been learning something new every day of my life and I have dedicated time to educating myself outside of the classroom. I take pride in being a sponge and absorbing as much information as possible, and I intend to keep learning new things for as long as I'm around. Some people earn their degrees and are happy to finally close the door on school and leave it in the past. I am constantly studying and testing myself, and I don't think my educational journey will ever end.

So if you ask me how I feel about education, in spite of my lack of a piece of paper saying that I have one, my answer is simple: I'm for it. I was thrilled to help my daughters plan their futures and I looked forward to watching them step out on their own as adults.

While all of this was going on, the doctors still couldn't figure out what was causing Heather's heart palpitations so they ordered a heart monitor for her to wear. She put it on the Friday before our camping trip, and of course went out of her way to hide it and not call attention to herself.

The following weekend Heather and I joined some close friends for a boat ride in the San Juan Islands. That Friday Heather removed the heart monitor and mailed it back for an evaluation. When the results came back we would meet with the cardiologist and try to figure out why she was having these issues. On Saturday morning we said goodbye to the girls, then met Ed and his wife Michele, our friends Dave and Janet, and Jerry and Shelly who owned the boat. We loaded the vessel with food, beer, wine, and water and set out from

Anacortes to Orcas Island where we planned to spend some time touring the Rosario resort before heading out again, this time to Lopez Island.

It was a picture-perfect day on the water, blue skies, no wind. Heather wasn't a big fan of boating, but she enjoyed herself and even piloted the boat during the second leg of the trip, from Orcas Island to Lopez Island.

We spent a couple hours on Lopez, had an early dinner and met up with some other friends who were also boating for the day. As we left Lopez and started back to Anacortes, our other friends decided to follow us back in their own boat.

After about fifteen minutes, all of the ladies settled into the main cabin to drink wine and socialize. Ed, Jerry and I were enjoying the beauty of the San Juan Islands from the flying bridge. It was peaceful, idyllic, serene.

Then, from below deck, Michele screamed my name. Ed and I bolted down the stairs and found Heather grasping at her chest, gasping for breath. We made eye contact. Then she passed out.

We started CPR and Jerry called the Coast Guard. Another friend from the other boat jumped aboard and helped with the CPR. A frantic and agonizing ninety minutes followed. The Coast Guard and a team of paramedics came on board to work on Heather. They labored without success for over an hour, but amazingly, only moments before they would be forced to stop performing CPR, they got a heartbeat. They summoned a helicopter for Heather, put me and Ed on a Coast Guard cutter, raced us to the mainland, and then to the hospital.

Heather's best friend, Shelly, was already in the waiting room when Ed and I got there. After everyone else arrived back on the mainland, Michele and Janet went to pick up our daughters, who were at home waiting for our return, completely unaware of everything that had occurred. At this point we still had hope. We had no idea what was going to happen.

When the helicopter finally arrived, the doctors did their assessment and gave us the news: They didn't think Heather was going to make it. I took a moment to choke back my emotions, and I told them to abide by the directives in her living will. After the girls arrived and were able to see their mother, the doctor pulled me aside and confirmed our worst fears: Heather would not make it through the night.

I have been through a lot of challenges in my life, but none of it prepared me for the heartbreak of telling my children that their mother would never come home.

In the early hours of the morning, on September 9th, 2012, at only forty-eight years old, Heather passed away with the girls and I, and some of our closest friends, by her side.

For years we had done our best to make family meals a priority, sharing dinner three to five days a week and discussing everything from what the girls were doing in school, to finances, and even death. Because of the open lines of communication in our family, and our willingness to talk about difficult issues, the girls knew exactly what to do. They planned a beautiful service to honor their mother. Heather was a giving and loving person who touched hundreds, if not thousands, of lives. Heather taught many people, including myself, the true value and blessing of life, the beauty of compassion and kindness, and the importance of serving others, among countless other lessons. We rented the local performing-arts center for her service. Over seven hundred and fifty people came to pay their respects and say farewell.

Chapter Nine

WE CARRY ON

How do you move on from this? I had been the family's driving force, but Heather was the glue that held everything together. I was the muscle, but she was the heart. I was at a loss, so I did what I had learned to do in every challenging situation: I buried myself in personal-development and counseling. Thank God I had great people at CPI and an amazing network of friends who were there for the girls and me when we needed them most.

At the company my managers and partners told me to take as much time as I needed. We had paid the union off only three months earlier, and they were doing an incredible job of running the company without me, just as good managers should. I had spent years developing a team that could run on autopilot if anything ever happened to me, and now I was happy to let them take the reins so that the girls and I could figure out how to build a new life for ourselves without Heather.

At home the girls wanted to get back to school as soon as possible and try to return to a sense of routine and normalcy. Ed and Kevin were—and are—the types of friends who only come around once in a lifetime. As I struggled, the one thing they knew would help was to keep me exercising and living a healthy lifestyle, and they saw to it that I did. Every day they showed up in their running clothes to take me for a run. Those first couple of weeks with Ed and Kevin were pivotal for me. They set the tone for the life that I would live after Heather's passing, and I believe it helped them, too. I've always been told that if I surrounded myself with good people good things would happen. Now, in one of the darkest moments of my life, I got to see that play out at work and at home.

About a month after Heather's death I finally decided to return to the office. I had stopped by a couple of times to check in, but I was in no frame of mind to return full-time. When I finally did, I found myself waiting for the staff to finish a company meeting. When they emerged, every one of them offered a hug and a "Welcome home." The love and support I received from my employees was overwhelming. How many business owners can say that they have a staff that is as devoted, competent, and loyal as the one at CPI? Not many.

A few weeks later I met with the cardiologist who examined Heather when she was having palpitations. I still didn't have a satisfactory diagnosis for what had happened and I wanted to get his input. He said that they couldn't agree upon a conclusive cause of death, even with all of the tests, the heart monitor, and the autopsy. He even took her results to a major cardiologist conference at the University of Washington to have multiple cardiologists read the results. After a long discussion, I told him it was okay; my belief was that she died from stress and anxiety. She had such a big heart and she always put everyone else before herself. No one's heart could give that much and have that much stress and live through it. And no amount of picking apart her test results would bring her back.

I also had a more personal reason to visit him. In 2010 he discovered that I had a defective aortic heart valve. He said that I could live with it for now, there was no immediate danger, but that it would need to be corrected after about five to eight years depending upon how things looked in the meantime. He said that things still looked good; come back in two more years and we'll see where you stand.

Those two years were a blur. My oldest daughter graduated from high school and, about a year after her mother's death, left for college, leaving only my youngest and myself. I continued to work out and run once or twice a day, often with Ed and Kevin who continued to keep me on track. We were also pretty competitive, always pushing each other to see what we could do next and what personal records we could break.

That's when Kevin came up with a hare-brained idea: Hike *Seven Lakes In Seven Hours*, in the Chuckanut mountain range close to where we lived, and call the whole thing *SLISH*. He said no one else had ever done it and that we should be the first.

He talked us into it. As we were planning and trying to figure out how to make the twenty-six-mile hike from lake to lake in only seven hours, word got out and people in the community started to hear about what we were up to. One day, while Kevin was at a meeting for the local hospital fundraising board, the director overheard him talking about it. They were getting ready to kick off a fundraising campaign for a new cardiac rehabilitation center for the hospital and asked him if we could turn SLISH into a fundraising opportunity. I was certainly in favor of helping out the hospital, but the clincher was when the director offered to name the new cardiac rehabilitation center after Heather. The idea of making such an important health-care facility into a living memorial to the most selfless person I had ever known was overwhelming. Of course I was all in and, after discussing it with Ed, Kevin, their wives, and my girls, I made a commitment to raise one hundred thousand dollars in five years and, if we accomplished that feat, the hospital would name the center after Heather.

So in 2014, two years after Heather's death, Ed, Kevin and his youngest daughter, another friend named Todd, and I began the trek through the mountains to connect seven lakes in seven hours. It was a beautiful September morning and we had it all planned out, the route we would take, the breaks, and when we would finish.

But nothing ever goes as planned. About halfway in we hit a little obstacle: Todd and Kevin's meticulous route planning and site visits didn't prepare us for the brand-new and unpredicted logging operation that knocked us off course (and lost) for about one and a half hours. After finally getting back on the trail, and way behind schedule, everyone said that making the journey in seven hours was now literally impossible so we may as well take our time and have fun. Don't tell me that something is literally impossible! Our fate was sealed the minute I heard that. Now there was no way that we weren't going to succeed. And above all else, we had accepted people's money with the promise that we would complete the hike within seven hours. We had a moral obligation to do so.

With no time to spare, we stopped hiking and started running. We challenged each other and pushed each other to sprint up and down the mountain, hitting all the lakes for photo ops, getting covered in sticker bushes and stinging nettles, and we finished the hike with only minutes to spare. The five of us raised thirty-five thousand dollars in seven hours, thirty-five percent of our five-year goal of one hundred thousand dollars. Not bad. Even better: After our success we were swamped with applications from people who wanted to join next year's hike.

A couple months later I had my follow-up appointment with the cardiologist. This time the hammer fell. The stress of losing Heather, raising our daughters alone, running the business, and working out a couple times a day had worsened my heart condition. He told me that I needed to prepare myself for surgery in the next year or two. To this point in my life I had never had any side effects or other issues that concerned me about my heart. Thank God for doctors.

In the spring of 2015 my youngest daughter graduated from high school and, when fall rolled around, she left for college. I was now officially an empty-nester. Things were still going well at CPI; the company was growing and making money, but more importantly, it had evolved. We had become a training organization as much as we were a plumbing company. With all of the personal development, counseling, and support for the company in the community, we wanted to give back and help others grow, too. We started a charity club at CPI and gave one percent of all revenue back to local charities. Each month, half of that one percent goes to the employee of the month to donate to the local charity of his or her choice. The other half stays in a separate account to give to selected local charities that need help. To date, CPI has given well over one hundred and fifty thousand dollars back to the local community.

On the personal-development front, Brad and I did some brainstorming about what new programs we could offer to the staff. One vital subject that many people never learn to master is financial literacy. I had always been good with money; even more so since I had sobered up and Steve started mentoring me. I had gotten so good at it that now, years later, I was financially free, a goal that most people never reach. I had taken Dave Ramsey's financial literacy course and found it pretty close to what Steve had taught me: save money for emergencies, don't borrow, avoid credit cards, pay off your house early. I figured I may as well become a Master Financial Coach through the Dave Ramsey Organization and teach the course myself.

After teaching the course to our employees and talking about the impact it was having, members of Service Roundtable started hearing about it. Not only did CPI win Plumbing Contractor of the Year at the 2013

Service Roundtable conference for prospering through the union challenges and Heather's death, but in 2014 we received what was then known as the George Brazil Trailblazer Award for the most innovative training. Not many companies in the home service industries or, for that matter, any companies at all, help and coach their employees with personal finances or will even talk with them about it, but then again I like to step out of my comfort zone, and Heather's death had changed my perspective on what was most important for my business and employees. More than ever I was aware of how much our employees depended upon me, personally, to ensure their livelihood and to help them be the best people they could be. Many companies, especially larger ones, have staff-development and enrichment programs, and many of those companies don't take it very seriously. While some do a fantastic job, far too many treat it as a nuisance, something that has to be crossed off of a list every year. I, on the other hand, had reached a point where I almost felt as if staff development was the most important part of my job. It was no longer simply about making the company as successful as it could be; it was about making my people as successful as they could be, as parents, employees, and human beings. If my people were successful, and equipped with the proper goals, knowledge, attitudes, and motivations, the company would take care of itself.

The second annual SLISH hike welcomed forty-five participants and we raised another thirty thousand dollars, bringing the total to over seventy thousand dollars—seventy percent of our five-year goal—in only two years.

Chapter Ten

HEARTSICK

A week after the second SLISH hike I set out for our vacation condo with seven other buddies for a guy's weekend that came to be known as *Fatcamp*. Ed, Kevin, and I were all big on intense physical activity and one morning we took it upon ourselves to run "The Hill," a road that leads from the main highway down to Crescent Bar and is one and a half miles up to the top at about a twenty-percent grade. When we got back down to the bottom we would usually walk to another short one-hundred-yard hill where we would race to the top, pushing ourselves to our limits, then walk the final two hundred yards back to the condo.

Kevin disappeared partway through the trek to "chase squirrels," as we liked to say. He had a habit of breaking away and doing his own thing, leaving me and Ed to finish on our own. It was grueling, as always, but that was the idea. There's no point in doing it if it's easy. It's the difficult things that change our lives and mold us into better people. As we started back to the condo I was stricken with an intense pain behind my ribs. I stopped, clutched at my chest, and struggled to breathe through it. I thought I was going to have the big one right there. Thank God I didn't, but I knew that my long-promised surgery wasn't far off.

That fall, with our fundraising efforts well ahead of schedule, the Heather Schols Cardiac Rehabilitation Center opened at the Skagit Valley Hospital. Seeing Heather's name on the wall, knowing that countless lives would be enhanced and improved through our efforts, was an overwhelming moment. Most importantly, it perpetuated Heather's own selflessness and concern for others. She always put everyone else before herself, and now a facility that bore her name would be a positive force in her own community by helping cardiac patients get their lives back on track. I can only imagine how happy she would have been to see it.

And, as if I needed another reminder, the event pushed me to finally bite the bullet and have my heart valve replaced. Since both of the girls were in college I wanted to plan the surgery around them so that there would be as little impact on them as possible. They had lost their mother just three years earlier to a heart condition, so I figured it wasn't going to be easy to watch their dad go in for open-heart surgery. Part of lessening the potential impact was to ensure that I was prepared for the worst-case scenario. I made sure that my finances were in order. I saw to it that the company was in good hands. I continued to work out and run every day. And on December 22nd 2015, during the girls' Christmas break, I went in for surgery in the best physical, financial, emotional, and spiritual shape of my life.

After about a six-hour surgery, which included having my aortic valve and part of my aorta itself replaced, I was on my feet and ready to start recovery within twenty-four hours. On Christmas day, just three days after surgery, I was released from the hospital and able to spend the holiday at home with the girls. I couldn't have done that if I had been out of shape, overweight, or depressed. I took my fitness, my diet, and my mental health seriously and I've never regretted a moment that

I've spent keeping myself in peak condition. It paid off. Every ounce of preparation contributed to my lightning-fast recovery.

While resting at home on December 27th I received an email from CPI's commercial project manager/estimator. After twenty-six years with us he was quitting, and his last day would be December 31st. He said he would help wrap up our ongoing commercial jobs, but he was ready to step away and start his own business. Normally I might have been a little alarmed, but it really didn't seem as important as it might have been because the drugs they had me on were a little harsh. I figured I would deal with it when I got back to the office, but thank God I had great partners, a great team, and—again—meticulous preparation helping to keep things rolling while I recovered.

Three weeks after surgery I walked into the Heather Schols Cardiac Rehabilitation Center and started my real rehab in the facility we had named after my late wife. After three months of rehab I was released to full activity, and a month after that was back to running three miles a day, wakeboarding, waterskiing, and generally pushing my limits in every way, just as I had always done.

Chapter Eleven

PASSING THE BATON

When I finally returned to CPI, Brad, Oly, and I planned a way forward after the sudden departure of our commercial project manager/estimator. After conducting a quick internal investigation we discovered why he had been in such a hurry to leave and we instantly cut all remaining ties. We also got entirely out of new construction, a process that we had begun years before, to focus one hundred percent on service and repair.

So onto another transition for CPI and what would also be a huge transition for me, Brad, and Oly. They were already running the day-to-day operations of the company, and I had been getting more involved in mentoring and helping other companies in our industry through Service Roundtable and The Blue Collar Success Group. By now I was really stepping out of my comfort zone. I had learned how short life really was, and that no one is guaranteed a single moment, so my motto became *plan for the future but live for the day,* and my life reflected it. I did two things that were probably two of my biggest fears in life. On my fiftieth birthday I went skydiving with my girls, Kevin, and his oldest daughter. For forty-eight years I had said, *Why the hell would anyone ever jump out of a safe airplane?* But now, instead of saying I won't do it, I can say that I've done it, and I did it with my daughters.

The other major fear was public speaking. As I said earlier, I am, by nature, an introvert and pretty shy until I get to know someone. Believe it or not, it's true. Public speaking is the most frightening thing an introvert can do and it scared the hell out of me.

My community is a small one and a lot of people knew parts of my story and what my family and business had been through. The world is full of people who share my own challenges and difficulties, and I knew I could help them by sharing my own personal journey and how I was able to overcome the obstacles that once stood in my way. If I wanted to do this, and if I wanted to expand my consulting and mentoring work, I would have to become a public speaker. That was the next step, and until I took that step I was about as far along as I could go. I looked at those who had built careers in the field of personal-development, people like Brian Tracy and Dave Ramsey, and realized that they all had one thing in common: They were public speakers. And public speaking is a skill that has to be consciously cultivated. I wasn't born with the desire to shoot my mouth off in front of a crowd and risk making an ass of myself (the old joke is "I'd rather be in the coffin than deliver the eulogy"). The thought scared me to death. It scares *most* people to death. But when I made up my mind to do it I discovered something amazing: I was good at it. And I enjoyed it. And it changed people's lives. I would never have known that if I hadn't forced myself to take yet another step out of my comfort zone. Now I speak as often as I can at events, clubs, and seminars, inspiring (I hope!) listeners about how they, too, can do what I do: blow through life's roadblocks and achieve success that exceeds your wildest expectations. Speaking was also a great way to get the message out about SLISH and raise more money. And it worked!

Through my talks, and being more active in the community, I reunited with Scott, an old friend from high school. We had wrestled together in my junior year when I briefly returned to competitive sports but we'd lost contact. He suffered from rheumatoid arthritis and it had gotten to a point where the doctors had reached the limit of what they could do to help, so he decided to go all natural and started a yoga studio to work on his mind and body, to help others do the same, and hopefully make a living in the process. His health improved, but the stress of running the studio and trying to make ends meet took a toll and he started going downhill again. After attending a special clinic in Mexico, he returned to find his business in a shambles. He wasn't sure he could continue it and stay healthy.

It occurred to me that I might be in a position to help. I offered to coach and mentor him and he agreed. I was determined to guide him to success. The next week I drove to the address he had given me: 121 South Spruce Street, Burlington, Washington. When I arrived I just sat in the car for a moment, looking at the storefront. Scott's yoga studio was at the very same address as the alcohol treatment facility where I had started to turn my life around years before. What are the odds of that happening? There are literally thousands of addresses in the local area and I wound up at this one for the second time. It was impossible not to think that this could be the start of another important chapter in my life. So it was with some sense of almost supernatural providence that I found myself crossing that threshold once again, this time in my brand-new role of consultant and mentor. Scott was ready for me; we got started right away. Through our hard work, and Scott's dedication, Quantum Health and Yoga is running smoothly, it's making money, and Scott has a healthy work/life balance. I still mentor him and I also practice yoga there whenever I'm in town.

By this time I had joined forces with Kenny, the Blue Collar Coach, and we were doing business deals together. I was still involved with CPI, but my focus was shifting ever more toward coaching and other ventures. Kenny was growing Blue Collar and said that, when I was ready, he wanted me to coach and train with Blue Collar full time. I liked the sound of that, a kind of passing of the baton.

Since my youngest daughter was still in college and didn't know what she would do when she graduated, I wanted to keep my roots in Skagit Valley. Besides, I still owned CPI and all of my lifelong friends were there, so I wasn't ready to make that move just yet. We also hadn't raised all of the money for the Heather Schols Cardiac Rehabilitation Center and I was determined to continue the annual SLISH hikes until we had fulfilled our fundraising commitment.

It didn't take long. On September 9th 2017, five years after Heather's death, we did the final SLISH hike and raised the rest of the money needed to fulfill our hundred-thousand-dollar obligation and then some. We raised a hundred and forty-three thousand dollars in just four years—more than we had promised and a year ahead of schedule. I never doubted that we could do it, but it was more successful than I ever imagined it would be.

Chapter Twelve

FULL CIRCLE

Brad and Oly were doing such a great job of running CPI that I didn't need to be there much and, honestly, my passions were increasingly elsewhere. I owned sixty-five percent of the company and they owned thirty-five percent between the two of them. At the beginning of 2018 I made a proposal: They could earn more stock in the company over the next three years if they hit a series of specific goals, set by me. If they hit those numbers each year for three years they would, together, own forty-nine percent of the company and I would retain fifty-one percent. At that point we would discuss a buyout. The catch was that, during this three-year period, I would only commit one week a month to CPI so that I could pursue my coaching and training programs and other ventures.

By October I had become completely disengaged at CPI and I had my first official coaching client. I spent three days in beautiful San Clemente, California working with Mike from Triton Heating and Air on his operations and finances, and doing a financial workshop for his employees. It was an all-inclusive deal for the management and staff.

When I returned to CPI for my one-week-a month contribution, Brad asked for a meeting with me. Knowing that I would only be there for a few short days he wanted to see to it that we got together before I left. As we sat down I could tell that something was bothering him. We had worked together for twenty-four years and we'd had our differences, but we also had a working relationship that most people can only dream about. After all of our time together, I could tell when Brad was afraid to say something that might ruffle my feathers. He would hesitate and stall, both of which he was doing now. I pushed him to tell me what was on his mind and he finally blurred it out: "What do we need to do to get you out of here? Oly and I want to buy you out and run the company by ourselves." He said that he and Oly figured they could run the company without me now; besides, they wanted to make improvements and didn't like waiting for my approval. He explained everything in the most delicate way he could to avoid offending me, until I finally I stopped him. I said, "You don't need to justify anything. If I were you guys I would want me out of here as well. Besides, as hard as it will be emotionally after being involved and running the company for twenty-nine years, it's your time to shine. I have done all I can and I've done everything I want to do here; it's time for you guys to take the company to another level."

By December 21st a buyout contract was in place and signed; it took effect December 31st 2018, Just a month after Brad asked to meet. Our phenomenal working and personal relationship meant that everything was in place at the company for a seamless succession.

When the handover was complete I asked Oly if he remembered what he had asked me a couple of years earlier about my involvement in the company: "Why do you need to do all this other stuff? Why don't you just focus on CPI and help us grow it?" I had told him that I could definitely do that and be involved in everything that is going on with CPI, but that doing so would slow Brad and Oly's growth and prevent them from being all that they could be. Only by letting them take the reins without me looking over their shoulders could they fulfill their greatest potential. Too many managers, whether intentionally or not, hold their people back. Some are afraid that their employees will leave and take their skills elsewhere; others have a subconscious fear of being surpassed by talented subordinates. I was able to succeed because I was given opportunities to expand beyond my narrowly defined workplace roles. The person who works in the field isn't supposed to help with accounting, but I did, and my supervisors did more than just tolerate my curiosity; they encouraged it. I fostered the same type of environment at CPI and I've seen it bear fruit.

And it doesn't end at the workplace. We all want to help our children be everything that they can be, but we're often afraid to let go and allow them to flourish. When my daughters had the chance to travel overseas I practically pushed them out the door. Was it hard to watch them go? Sure. But I knew that they would learn far more in a few short months than they could by staying put at home. Both have studied abroad and traveled the world; they've done volunteer work in Africa, Thailand, and the Dominican Republic. They gained an understanding of global cultures and peoples that can't be taught in a textbook, they have a greater appreciation of their own country's blessings and opportunities, and they acquired an unstoppable self-confidence and autonomy.

I may not have sent my employees overseas, but I gave them every other opportunity that I could to evolve and change and grow. I think my highest calling is to help develop others to the point that they are better people than I am. That is the greatest reward that I can receive.

So it was time to let Brad and Oly fly. Letting go can be one of the hardest things you ever do in business. It's just like saying goodbye to your kids when you send them away to college. And, just like the proud father that I am, I couldn't more proud of Brad and Oly and the work that they are doing with CPI.

Now, for the first time in twenty-nine years, I didn't have a job to go to or a company of my own. I had invested in real estate and, with the buyout, have created ample residual income and am completely debt free. However, I'm not one to sit around and do nothing, so I rented a place in Arizona and live there part-time so I can be more involved in business and financial coaching with Kenny and Blue Collar.

I've been coaching Mike with Triton Heating and Air every week since doing the three-day onsite program with him and his team. During one of our calls we discussed his plan for 2019 and the future of Triton. He said he had a plan but had never done a planning and strategy meeting with his management team. If you have a business or family, I suggest meeting at least once a year to plan and dream about the future, to decide what you want it to look like, what it will take to make it happen, and to commit to accomplishing it. This is how businesses and families succeed and rise above the levels that most people consider to be satisfactory. Are you satisfied with where your life is now? If so, ask yourself if you would be happier if things were even better. Would you be? Of course you would. They *can* be. The key to getting there is to meet, brainstorm, establish goals, and make plans to achieve them. Do that once a year, take it seriously and follow through, and you'll be amazed at the progress you make in a few short years. You can be comfortable where you are, or you can be extraordinary, and have the business—and live the life—of your dreams. I choose to follow my dreams and I'm going to help as many other people as I can to follow theirs.

So it was time for Mike to host a planning and strategy meeting with his staff to chart a course for the future of his company. I told him I would help him facilitate everything, and that I thought we should do the meeting offsite so we could focus on the task at hand without the distractions and interruptions of the workplace. On January 23rd 2019 I drove from Arizona to San Clemente, a beautiful little beach town in southern Orange County, California. I got there the night before so I could get a good night's rest and be ready to lead. The next morning I went for a run. The last time I was there, during the three-day onsite meeting, I had found a breathtaking trail that runs along the Pacific Ocean. What better way to get my mind right for the busy day ahead?

As I ran I visualized what lay ahead, where we would do the meeting, and how the day would unfold, getting my mind right. Mike trusted me to guide him to the future and I was determined to deliver all the value I could.

When I arrived at the Triton office, Mike told me that we would be meeting at a clubhouse owned by his office manager's dad. It was a short drive away. "Wonderful," I thought. "Let's go!"

I had no idea where we were going or what was about to happen, but I was excited to be able to help. As I jumped in my car to follow Mike out of the parking lot, little did I know that the one who would get the most help would be me.

As we wound our way down to the Pacific Coast Highway all I could think was, *Where the hell are we going?* As we turned north on the Pacific Coast Highway I thought maybe we'd head toward Dana Point, which was the next little beach town north of San Clemente. I was wrong. We kept driving. I truly had no clue where we were going, and I was getting concerned about how much valuable time we were wasting in our cars looking at the scenery.

Then we turned off of the Pacific Coast Highway and on to Laguna Canyon Road. As we rolled along the canyon I was overcome with a powerful sensation of peace and tranquility that I had never felt before. When we arrived at the clubhouse, and I got out of the car, Mike could tell something wasn't right. He asked me if everything was okay. I got emotional. I could feel the tears welling up in my eyes, my cheeks flushing. I said, "I left this canyon twenty-nine years ago not knowing where my life was going. I was dead broke, an alcoholic, and had no direction. I said that I would never come back here. But here I am. I have come full circle. And my life has changed in every way imaginable. Now, twenty-nine years later to the week, I am back in this canyon teaching you and your team what I spent the last three decades learning the hard way. What worked for me will almost certainly work for you; and while it may not be easy, it will definitely be worth it. Let's get started."

Chapter Thirteen

FINAL THOUGHTS

In the years since Heather's death, many people have asked me how I got through it all, along with everything else in my life, and flourished while doing it. As you can see from this book, it hasn't always been easy. I have thrived when others have failed, and I have zoomed ahead where others have stalled. It isn't because there's anything special about me. It's because I've been through a lot and, crucially, I learned from it, asked for help when needed, changed my behaviors, and sought to improve myself in every way that I could while helping others to do the same. My experiences, good and bad, along with Heather's death, have taught me a lot about myself and how short life can be. It has made me a better, more understanding, more giving person; more importantly, it has helped the whole community and, through the Heather Schols Cardiac Rehabilitation Center, will continue to do so long after I'm gone.

People say they can't imagine what my girls and I have been through. I say surround yourself with good people and remember that can't never did anything anyway.

THE 10 RENEGADE LAWS
OF SUCCESS

I was born with some good traits and some bad ones, and I've worked to amplify the former and diminish the latter. I've learned a lot of lessons and gained tremendous wisdom, sometimes easily, sometimes through heartache and tragedy, and sometimes in spite of me fighting back tooth and nail, but in the end the only things that count are that I learned, I changed, and I grew. Some of what I've learned has been hard won, but it doesn't have to be for you. In reading this book you can see the circumstances that led me to adopt successful traits without having to learn all of them the hard way yourself. You can have the gain without the pain, but only if you take the lessons to heart and make them work for you. And bear this in mind: every item on this list is an essential ingredient in my success. Remove one of them and the story turns out differently. Learn these lessons, remember them and, most importantly, apply them. I hope they make as much difference in your life as they've made in mine.

WORK HARD

Hard work is the single bedrock common denominator of my success. Without understanding the value of hard work nothing else would have been possible. This is one trait that I feel I was born with, and an important component of it is a simple desire to please. I cannot stand to let someone down. That's why I spent hard hours throwing hay bales and mucking out sewage in a hospital crawlspace.

Aside from earning a living, one of the greatest benefits of hard work is one that I only grew to understand in hindsight: It was my unwavering work ethic that built my reputation among those who enabled me to move to ever higher levels of success. It was why Dennis offered me a job with Purves plumbing—one of my life's pivotal events—and why Steve wanted me to come back to Washington and work with him at CPI. How many people can say they've been hounded to come and work for someone? Steve did it because my work ethic was legendary and he wanted someone like me on his team.

And, from where I stand today, I can tell you that every hour of hard labor that I endured has paid off handsomely. It will do the same for you. Many of us feel the temptation to slack off, but the world is filled with slackers. Be the exception. Be the person who everyone wants on their team.

And one last thing: There are plenty of people out there with greater gifts and higher knowledge than I have, but there aren't many who work harder. The person who works harder is the one who will succeed. Hard work trumps talent every time.

SET GOALS

Goals are the shining beacons that guide us to wherever it is we wish to go. When you set a goal your life acquires a purpose that was missing before. Without goals your life is rudderless, and the only things you're working for are the next bedtime, the next paycheck, the next slice of pizza. What kind of life is that? When you choose a goal, and you chart a course to achieve it, all of the Netflix movies and the mornings spent sleeping in late will start to seem like nuisances. How can you spend hours watching television when there's a goal to be accomplished?

Early in my working life I set a personal goal to become a millionaire. That goal never left my mind, and there were days that it kept me working long after everyone else had thrown in the towel. And I reached my goal! I did it without even having a clear strategy (I did get better at this), but the simple fact of having that goal, always on my mind, always dangling before me, kept me motivated and focused on something that was specific and attainable. We become what we spend most of our time thinking about. Hey, I'm a millionaire plumber. Not bad. What goals can *you* accomplish?

SEIZE OPPORTUNITIES

This is the domain of *coulda, shoulda, woulda.* Over a lifetime, how many opportunities do we turn down? For most of us, it's a lot. Why do we turn them down? Usually it's one of two things: fear or comfort. The opportunity is either too scary (I could never do that!) or we're too comfortable where we are (things are good; I'm not budging).

When I was offered the opportunity to work with Purves Plumbing I was faced with fear and uncertainty. The only thing I knew about plumbing was how to turn the faucet knob. But I took the plunge anyway and everything that's happened to me since is predicated on that one decision: I am phenomenally successful because I took a leap of faith into the unknown. I could have listened to my fears and built a career throwing hay. I'm glad I didn't. You shouldn't, either.

And I don't mean that you should be irresponsible. After all, I also once seized the opportunity to jump from a hotel balcony into a swimming pool. Think about the opportunity and, if you feel some trepidation, ask yourself why. Is it because you lack knowledge or experience? Because you'll fail? If so, I understand. I felt the same way. But I've learned that the best way to gain knowledge and experience is to *gain knowledge and experience*. And the only way to do that is to seize the opportunity, take it seriously, and get to work. Keep your mind open and your hands busy and you will not fail.

Or maybe it isn't really fear that holds you back. Maybe you're too comfortable where you are. Steve asked me to come and work with him at CPI when I was enjoying the high life in southern California. Bad timing on his part. I loved where I was and I did not want to leave. It was easier to stay. I was comfortable. I could have remained where I was, enjoyed the sand and the sun, and kept on partying with my friends. I could also still be working with the tools at job sites every day, making a tiny fraction of my eventual income, and never acquiring ownership of a fantastic company. Thank God Steve wouldn't leave me alone, and I eventually came around to seize one of the greatest opportunities of my life.

Don't let opportunities pass you by. Don't live a life of regret wondering what could have happened if you had taken that chance. Evaluate the possibilities, push fear and comfort to the side, and *take that chance*. A once-in-a-lifetime opportunity only comes around—you guessed it—once in a lifetime, and Steve is no longer in the business of pestering people. *Seize your opportunities* and take your life to a new level with bold new possibilities.

BE ADAPTABLE: CHANGE

I am not the person I used to be. Sure, I still have some of the same traits, mostly the good ones (I hope), but through experience and some hard knocks I've learned to cast off the things that were destructive to myself and others.

They say that the leopard never changes its spots. I disagree. I have changed enormously—for the better—

and so can you. Too many people get set in their ways and never even consider the fact that, with just a few changes in behavior and attitude, they could be completely different, and better, people. Even worse, some people take pride in their immovability. "This is the way I am and this is the way I'm staying!" You could never do a greater disservice to yourself. Look at your life, have the courage to be honest about what you see, and have the will to change what doesn't work. The fundamental changes that I made in my life, especially confronting my alcoholism, affected me, my family, and my coworkers in deep and profound ways. I can't imagine where I would be right now if I had been too stubborn to change.

WATCH YOUR MONEY

This might seem awfully nuts-and-bolts compared to some of the other high-minded topics on this list, but it's no less essential. Keeping yourself on sound fiscal footing is a key to ongoing success, and you don't have to be a financial wizard to do it. It's as simple as this: Spend less than you make. Investments, stocks, savings plans, etc., are all well and good, but my most crucial advice, without which nothing else is possible, remains the same: *Spend less than you make.*

It's obvious, right? *Spend less than you make.* What could be simpler? *Spend less than you make.* Yet the world is filled with people who won't follow that simple rule, and many of them are up to their ears in debt and riddled with the stress that comes from having to pay today for yesterday's bad habits. All of which could be avoided if only they had remembered to... Well, you get the picture.

And remember, I fell off this wagon once. When I was in southern California I gave in to the temptation of buying fancy, expensive things and trying to keep up with others who were doing the same. That, combined with my expensive partying lifestyle, was a degenerative cycle that spiraled out of control until I was no longer able to pay my own rent in spite of the fact that I was making decent money. I pulled myself out of that mess and I never let it happen again.

And if you're in the habit of outspending your income, don't think for a minute that getting a raise will solve your problem. You will simply increase your spending to match your raise and still be in the same boat. You have to actively commit to reducing your spending; only then can you begin to become financially secure and start taking the other steps, like investments and savings vehicles, that can help you build a rock-solid future for you and your family.

LEARN ALL THAT YOU CAN

I didn't do well in school and I never went to college, yet I place a high value on knowledge and education. Throughout my life I have taken every opportunity to learn something new at every job I've ever held; in fact, I learned more through on-the-job training than I ever did in school, and I'm not just talking about learning a trade. I learned psychology, economics, business, mathematics, communications, and a host of other disciplines, all while down in the trenches earning a paycheck.

It's one thing to be exposed to all of this education; it's another to be conscious of it and understand how your everyday experiences are changing your life. At Purves Plumbing I learned every aspect of the business and sought to make myself someone who could jump into any role and do whatever was required at any given time. It made me one of the company's key employees; someone who was called upon time and again to help someone out of a tight spot. And my ceaseless thirst for learning continues to bring me new opportunities. Every new experience I have is a key, and every key I have opens a new door.

Your education didn't end on the last day of school. On the contrary, the day you graduated was the beginning of the best class you'll ever attend. Education is vision and you should never be satisfied with the view from where you stand. Learn more, seek new knowledge and skills, and your horizons will expand farther than you would ever have thought possible.

BELIEVE IN YOURSELF

Self-confidence is paramount. If you believe in yourself, and are clear about what you do and don't want, you will have the gumption to jump into the middle of a difficult situation and do what needs to be done. When I was young I had little doubt in my abilities. I knew I could be a top player on any team and my belief in myself gave me the confidence that I needed to prove it. And I did prove it, time and time again. My self-confidence helped me succeed in business; without it I never could have taken those first crucial steps into the world of plumbing when I didn't even know a thing about it.

Sometimes self-confidence comes down to a little bit of psychological sleight of hand. In other words, you might have to talk yourself into it. That's okay. Self-confidence didn't always come easily to me, I have had to talk myself into it many times; to some it's one of the most difficult things to accomplish. Always remind yourself that people with no more skill and talent than you have take leaps of faith every day and succeed. If they can do it, you can do it; and if you don't do it, *someone else is going to do it instead of you.* Don't let that happen. Get clarity, muster up the confidence and make it work for you. You've got this.

I wish it were exactly that simple, but there is one complication. Even someone like me, for whom self-confidence seems to come more naturally than most, can suffer from a crisis of confidence. When I was in California and Steve was trying to recruit me to work with him at CPI, it wasn't just the sun and the sand that held me back. My drinking and partying and financial issues had eroded my self-confidence. I no longer felt like I could surmount any problem through hard work and determination. Instead I felt as if I had maxed out and my best days might be behind me. It's an awful thing to have to come to terms with when you're not used to self-doubt, but Steve saw who I was and what I was capable of, in spite of my temporary problems, and I will always be grateful to him for that. With his help I was able to restore my self-confidence and I've never let it slip since.

So, as with financial responsibility, I have been on both sides of the self-confidence issue. When I had clarity I have succeeded and when I didn't have clarity I have failed. And it's because I have dropped the ball and recovered, in both areas, that I have the confidence to tell you that you can do the same even if you're at rock bottom. I've been there and I've done it. You can, too.

GET OUT OF YOUR COMFORT ZONE

If you want something better than what you've got—in any area of life—you have to step out of your routine and do the things that make you nervous, uncomfortable, or uneasy. If you never take that step you will never move past where you are.

I know it's not easy. I did it when I joined Purves Plumbing in spite of knowing nothing about plumbing, I did it when I started selling cars in spite of never having worked in automotive sales, and I did it when I started public speaking in spite of never having addressed a group of strangers. Each of these was an excruciating, nerve-wracking experience—at first. In each case, the idea of doing something new was far worse than the reality. I quickly found my groove, did well, and enjoyed it. I blew the doors off of the plumbing business, I was a top salesman at the car dealership, and I am killing it as a public speaker. I stepped into each of these fields without knowing the first thing about any of them. And in each case I succeeded.

What uncomfortable things could you be doing right now to enhance your career? (Hint: Public speaking skills will enhance *any* career). Get out there and do it. And remember: Whatever it is, you can't know less about it than I did.

FOCUS ON YOUR FAMILY AND GIVE BACK TO THE COMMUNITY

I have a complicated family history and I don't think I fully appreciated what family could mean until I started to build one of my own. Family expands your sense of self. You begin to realize, in a real and tangible way, that everything you do is done for an entity larger than yourself, and one that will ultimately outlive you. It gives you a sense of purpose, drive, and momentum that will surpass anything that you have ever known, and you will work secure in the knowledge that everything you accomplish supports those who will, in turn, support you.

147

Life is short. As time passes I understand that everything that I have done, and everything that I do, has ultimately become aligned with my family. Family keeps me sane, grounded, and whole. And it helps me maintain a healthy perspective on what my role is in the world. Which brings me to my next point.

Your community is your extended family. They taught you in school, they supported you when you were growing up, they were there to help you when things went wrong. They are your friends, your neighbors, your customers. We are all connected and, even though we may not realize it, the success or failure of one of us affects all of us. I became involved in my community purely out of self-interest: I was trying to get a more lenient DUI sentence from Mr. Mullen. But as with so many other things, when I got involved I jumped in one hundred percent and it changed my life.

Now community giving is an integral part of the business at CPI. It is hardwired into the company and, as far as I'm concerned, it always will be. I started doing financial counseling at CPI because I wanted to help our employees. I didn't have to do that; in fact, I know few others who do. But I see the good that it's done and the positive effects that sound financial literacy has set in motion throughout the CPI family. SLISH brought the whole regional community together in a very real way to raise money for a facility that will, in turn, benefit the whole regional community. And here's the thing: All of the things that I did, even SLISH, which raised well over a hundred thousand dollars, could have been done without spending a dime. All it takes is a little time and vision. No excuses. How can you start impacting your community today?

BLOW THROUGH THE NAYSAYERS

Can't never did anything. Sadly, there always seems to be someone who's only too happy to tell us what we can't do. It's easy to let them get you down and discourage you. *They're right. There's no way I can do this and I was crazy to think that I could.* Don't fall for it! You can accomplish amazing things far beyond what you think you're capable of and your secret weapon is right there between your ears. I think back to that Little League coach telling us that we weren't ready for the big time, and you know what? I am so glad that he doubted us. I am glad that he told us we couldn't do it. He gave me a great gift: the opportunity to prove him wrong. I wish I could buy him a new car and a box of chocolates, because his doubts sowed the seeds for where I am today. I proved him wrong, I've been proving naysayers wrong ever since, and I'll prove some more wrong tomorrow.

When someone tells you you're not good enough, you're not talented enough, you're not smart enough, you lack the vison or the know-how or the gumption, tell them "Thank you for giving me what I need to succeed," and then *prove them wrong*. Let those doubts fuel your passion and lead you to places you've never been before. I did it. People do it every day. *You can do it too.*

ACKNOWLEDGMENTS

I would like to thank my late wife Heather for giving me two beautiful daughters and for the twenty-two years we spent together. You made me a better, more compassionate person, willing to look at my faults, address them, and change for the better. You were taken away from us way too early but I will never forget your sweet nature, kind soul, and beautiful, playful spirit.

To my daughters, you two are the light of my life and I could not be prouder of the young women you have become. Thank you for always trying to keep me grounded and responsible.

To my mom who always told my brothers and me that we could do and accomplish anything we wanted to in life and that "can't never did anything."

To my brother Mark Schols who probably knows me better than anyone and has always been there for me.

Thank you for not only being a brother but a mentor as well, someone who will call me out on my bullshit and show me another way of looking at things.

To my brother Mike Schols for showing me the meaning of hard work and never giving up.

To my two best friends, Ed and Kevin:

Ed Perry has been with me in the darkest moments of my life as well as the brightest. Thank you for being you, supporting me no matter what, and never judging me.

Kevin Bingham has always pushed me to stay in shape, enjoy the moments, and have fun.

To my mentor, ex-business partner, and most importantly my friend, Steve Olsen. Thank you for believing in me and giving me the opportunity of a lifetime even when I didn't believe in myself. God only knows where I would have ended up without your guidance, mentoring, and friendship.

To my last business partners and friends, Brad Tully and Michael "Oly" Olsen, thank you for believing in my vision and following me in business and life. I could not be prouder of the men you guys are and how you are continuing the legacy at CPI. Thanks for allowing me to pursue my dreams, passions, and goals.

To Kenny and Christy Chapman for encouraging me to write this book and tell my story. And to Kenny for always challenging me to look deep inside myself for more.

To Mark Matteson who also encouraged me to write this book and pushed me to get out of my comfort zone. Without your encouragement this book may have never happened.

To the Skagit Valley community, the rest of my friends, and present and past employees at CPI, thank you for supporting me, my family, and business for all those years.

To Jason Liller, thank you for putting up with my bullshit and taking my manuscript and actually making it a work of art that I hope will reach and help a lot of people.

Kelly Schols is an author, inspirational speaker, success mentor, business consultant, and coach who draws upon his diverse industry knowledge and broad experience, from the field to the back office to the boardroom, to help executives and entrepreneurs trans-form their personal, professional, and financial goals into reality. His history of running a multi-million-dollar company, initiating revolutionary programs to encourage employee welfare and engagement, and dramatically exceeding his personal financial goals, all in spite of a rough-and-tumble youth spent in the school of hard knocks, enable him to help others climb to their own highest potential.

A widower and father of two daughters, Kelly spearheaded the effort to raise funds to establish the Heather Schols Cardiac Rehabilitation Center, named after his late wife, in Mount Vernon, Washington. He lives in Washington State where he pursues his mission to lead others to lives of success and significance.

Made in the USA
Columbia, SC
09 November 2020